Dark Psychology Manipulation

Highly Effective Techniques for Influencing People Using Mind Control, Persuasion, NLP and Deception-The Subtle Art of Brainwashing

Table of Contents

Introduction

Have you ever been in a situation where you needed someone to listen to you? Perhaps you were at a job interview, desperate to get hired for this job because you need to make sure you can pay all the bills. You may have sat there, wishing you had a way to sway the other person to see you as a valuable asset. Maybe you wished you could literally control the mind of the other person.

Well, today is your lucky day, because this book is here to tell you that you *can* control the minds of other people. Perhaps not in the sci-fi TV show sense, where you are controlling every little aspect of the other person's behaviors, but you absolutely can influence the way most people think, act, and feel. Through the skills developed and studied through dark psychology, you can master the art of manipulating and persuading people into doing whatever it is that you want them to do, and with that skill, you can make everyone around you as malleable as clay. With these skills mastered, you will eventually be able to control the behaviors of those around you, convincing them of whatever suits your needs best at that particular moment.

This book will delve into the art of dark psychology, taking the behaviors and manipulation tactics favored by those with a dark personality to predatorily identify, stalk, and hunt their targets with ease. These dark skills, though they can be incredibly harmful and insidious, can also be used in ways that can boost your rapport, granting you the advantage that could be the difference between sinking or swimming at your next job interview, the next time you are attempting to close on a deal, or even at your next first date.

Throughout these pages, you will learn all about dark psychology, delving into what it is, how it is used, and what exactly can make it so dangerous. You will be taught how to understand and read the body language of others, which will serve you well as you make your way through life, attempting to get only the best results as you do so. You will learn all about several different tactics that manipulators tend to prefer, ranging from covert emotional manipulation to dark seduction. Within each topic, you will be provided with the key components of each concept, any background information you will need, and several examples or steps involved in each concept, providing you with a comprehensive guide to everything you will need to know in order to manipulate, persuade, or control those around you. Lastly, you will be granted several ways to make yourself less vulnerable to each of the several techniques provided within this book to ensure that you never fall victim to the very techniques you are seeking to master.

As you go on this journey, discovering the arts of manipulating those around you, make sure to remember that this book does not endorse the use of these techniques to intentionally hurt others, neither physically nor emotionally. Each of these techniques can be used in very detrimental ways that can cause lifelong damage to those who fall victim to the techniques. As cliché as it is, remember that with the power that you will be gaining through this book, also comes the responsibility to use the information in intelligent, respectful manners that do not victimize everyone around you.

Chapter 1: Defining Dark Psychology

When you learn about psychology in school, you are introduced to a whole new world. You learn all about how the brain, perhaps the most complicated organ within the human body, functions, and ultimately, everything that everyone does is eventually broken down into nothing but electrical impulses created by neurons that are passed on to other neurons, and the entire impulse eventually spreads enough to create the action, feeling, thought, or sensation that you become aware of. Every complicated bit of yourself, your decisions on what to do or say, or how you feel when you see a certain person, can be explained by those same neurological impulses, no matter what the sensation. It is, at its simplest, the way that the body passes information from place to place. Despite how daunting and complicated humans may seem, we are actually surprisingly simple.

Humans follow a surprisingly simple sequence of thoughts, feelings, and behaviors, which feed into each other in a constant loop, with thought influencing how one feels, which influences one's actions, which in turn again influence their thoughts. When you understand that constant cycle, you will begin to recognize that it is surprisingly simple to hijack a person's mind. That is where dark psychology comes into play.

What is Dark Psychology?

Dark psychology takes an understanding of how people's minds work, understanding their most intrinsic, unconscious motivations, and using them. By understanding what motivates a person to behave in certain ways, regardless of whether it is in a positive or negative manner, you can take control of the person, preying on those motivations and turning them into something that can be influenced.

Those with the darkest personalities seem to understand this process innately, recognizing exactly how to identify a target, read a target, and ultimately, snare a target without needing a guide. Their own predatory instincts are honed naturally, making them incredibly effective at what they do. Dark psychology recognizes that those with dark personalities, narcissists, sadists, or psychopaths, seem to be inherent masters at manipulating others, usually managing to stay behind the scenes as they do so. These masters of manipulation are so skillful that no one ever suspects that they are doing what they are doing until it is too late and the damage is done. They utilize their inherent understanding of psychology and how it works in order to manipulate others, getting the results they need and making it seem effortless in the process.

Psychologists recognize these skills, seeking to further understand the process of manipulating other people, in breaking someone down so thoroughly that they are no longer someone they recognize in the mirror, and how they do so in ways that are so sneaky that they are frequently entirely overlooked. Psychologists recognize that this potential, this propensity to behave in ways that harm or control others, resides within each and every person in the world, though the vast majority of us keep it under lock and key. Every person around you has the potential to be a monster, behaving in ways that are harmful simply for the sake of predatory behavior.

However, psychologists have also come to recognize that, with the right motivations behind your actions, these dark psychology skills can be used for a myriad of good reasons. It can offer a defense—when you understand it, you are less susceptible to the tactics utilized. It can offer the skills that lead you to success when persuading people to give you better jobs or to take a chance with you. It can provide you the skills necessary to ensure that you are a better friend and family member. Psychologists have come to understand that just because you are using the same skills as those within the dark triad or with other dark personality types does not mean that you, yourself, must also give in to the darkness. You can take a look into the darkness without succumbing to it, allowing you to gain valuable skills that can be utilized to your benefit without becoming a predatory monster.

Principles of Dark Psychology

Those who utilize dark psychology frequently persuade, manipulate, deceive, coerce, seduce, and control the people around them. They want what they want and do not care about the cost. To them, the ends justify the means, even if the means they are using to reach that end are the wellbeing and happiness of those around them. To many of those within the dark triad, the only person whose happiness matters is their own. They may even be thrilled by hurting other people, gaining pleasure out of the suffering of those around them.

Oftentimes, those who are acting out in ways that utilize dark psychology techniques do so out of impulse—something in their unconscious encourages them to do so, so they do it with no regards to the consequences. They may see the other person as innately weaker than them, choosing to target them much like how a wolf would target weaker deer. They seek to make those that are weaker than them their prey. This is likely due to evolutionary instinct. Humans have three driving instincts that are massive motivators to their behaviors, culminating into what is referred to as the biological imperative, or the purpose of life in general: Sex, aggression, and self-preservation. These are quite self-explanatory: Sex is for procreation, allowing for genetics to pass through the generation. Aggression allows for protection of territory, the self, and mates, and self-preservation is the instinct to ensure survival at all costs.

Those who give in to dark psychology are typically acting upon one of these, either wanting to preserve the falsified images of themselves that they have been wearing like a mask, alleviate the aggressive drives they feel, or coerce someone into fulfilling sexual desires. However, the vast majority of people recognize that such devious, harmful methods have to be used in order to ensure survival. Most people recognize the constraints of society and live within them, knowing that their biological imperatives can still be achieved and fulfilled.

Though the dark psychology wielder is likely to be aggressive, he will still be tactful in his targets, seeking out the weakest targets that are the least likely to hurt them back in return. The same biological imperatives that encouraged them to lash out in the first place also restrain them to an extent, causing them to want to remain hidden and the only way they can remain hidden is if they remain unchallenged. For that reason, they seek out those who are the least likely to attempt to challenge them.

Ultimately, dark psychology can be identified by the following five traits:

- It is universal: Every human being has the potential for dark psychology manipulation within them, and every human being shares the potential to behave in violent and predatory manners

- It studies the way people think and feel, as well as how willing they are to utilize their understandings of the world to target other human beings

- It recognizes a spectrum of behaviors, with some behaviors being deemed as worse or more dark or evil than others

- That same spectrum is dependent upon how evil or inhumane the intentions behind the action were

- Understanding dark psychology allows for it to be controlled or restrained, while also recognizing just how useful dark psychology principles can be.

Examples of Dark Psychology

Imagine that you have just landed a job selling houses. You want to be successful at it, but recognize that it is a huge purchase for the vast majority of people, taking up a massive amount of money and requiring a long-term commitment. You also know that the more expensive the house you sell is, the more money you get, and the happier you are with your larger commission check. You then decide to learn how to persuade people and influence them with your body language to convince your clients to buy houses that are always just slightly outside of their original suggested max price they were willing to pay. This is dark psychology, appealing to dark persuasion techniques as well as using body language to influence.

Perhaps you are in an interview and you are asked a question that you cannot answer honestly without tanking your chances at getting the job. You instead utilize the art of deception, subtly sidestepping the issue altogether while also utilizing some of the techniques you learned about how to use mind games to completely distract the interviewer. You then skip over the question altogether, saving yourself the hassle of answering.

Maybe you are interested in getting someone to love you, but they will not give you the time of day. Through understanding persuasion tactics as well as how to seduce people, you can essentially hijack the other person's mind, making the other person interested enough to give you the chance to earn their love. Through skills such as knowing how to make yourself seem more interesting than most would give you credit for, to understanding just how to utilize eye contact to force an intimate connection, you will find your luck with those who interest you skyrocketing as you learn how to portray yourself and how to seduce successfully.

All of these are ways that dark psychology could be used to get the results you want with relatively little effort. Understanding the art of dark psychology can make walking through life a breeze, allowing you to shortcut your way to success, love, power, and anything else you wanted out of life. From here, you will begin to look at the wide array of ways that dark psychology can be utilized in order to lead the life you want to live.

Chapter 2: Dark Psychology Usage Today

Dark psychology is not just for people to use on an individual level—several larger corporations will utilize dark psychology tactics in a wide range of situations. Through understanding what makes the human mind tick, they are able to tap into the secrets of dark psychology, creating more appealing, more convincing, and more seemingly-honest organizations in an attempt to appeal to mass audiences all at once.

Dark Psychology in Media

The media is perhaps one of the most surprising aspects for many people when learning about dark psychology and its usage. People assume that the news and other media is reporting facts to the masses, rather than twisting it to ensure a buy, a click, or a view of a video. Remember, the media is one big business. All it cares about is lining its own pockets at the expense of you, the consumer. They will do anything to create a compelling story, even if that means utilizing methods used in psychology and dark psychology to do so.

News anchors and reporters will utilize body language tricks to sway the mood of whatever it is they are reporting on. Newspaper articles will use words that are meant to evoke feelings within you that can sway how you are reading it, particularly in the headlines in an attempt to get you drawn in as quickly as possible to get you as interested as possible as early as possible.

Magazines and newspapers will lead with headlines that draw in your attention quickly and effectively, seeking to get you to make an impulse buy when whatever it was that was written catches your eye.

Ultimately, all aspects of media only care about selling to you, and it is not afraid to utilize underhanded psychology and mind games in order to get the result it wants. There is a reason people always reiterate that you should never trust what you read online or see on television—it is because the media does not care about the viewers beyond making sure they are viewing.

Dark Psychology in Law

Particularly when an issue goes to trial, lawyers on both sides will utilize dark psychology in order to sway the judge or a jury to believe what is being said. Everything from body language to the way questions are answered, or not answered, all depend upon dark psychology and the methods used within it in order to get the necessary results.

Remember, in criminal law, a person cannot be charged if evidence brought by a prosecutor does not incriminate a person unless the conclusion the evidence implied is beyond a reasonable doubt. Because of this, defense attorneys will use anybody's language necessary to make people feel a doubt that will be enough to throw the case. The prosecutor will be doing the same, attempting to sway the people to believe beyond a doubt that the defendant is guilty. This leads to attorneys that come across as incredibly confident about two completely opposite positions.

Dark Psychology in Politics

Politics is all about convincing people to side with you. At the root, that is all that matters—getting enough votes to sway what is or is not acceptable in the eyes of the law. Politicians know that ultimately, the people do have at least some sort of say of what goes on within the country, whether it is reelecting the people in office or voting for or against some measure that was brought to the ballot. Because politicians must be able to keep the votes or get the votes they want or need, they oftentimes utilize principles found in dark psychology. They will wield the principles of persuasion against the masses; they will utilize emotions to get the results they want. They will use body language that makes them appear authoritative as they speak, saying exactly what the people want to hear with just enough ambiguity to ensure that they are not lying at the end of the day. Politicians are the ultimate manipulators, capable of convincing people to believe whatever they want. There is a reason that those who understand this stuff think of politicians as dishonest and snakes—it is because they are utilizing their understanding of dark psychology in order to manipulate people into doing their bidding.

Dark Psychology in Sales

Those who work in sales know exactly how important it is to close on sales—oftentimes, the bulk of the salesperson's income comes from commissions or bonuses that are only generated if they manage to make the sales necessary to get them. They are oftentimes entirely dependent on that income, especially in this day and age when minimum wages are not enough to get anything. Because of this, salespeople become good at reading people, utilizing the principles of persuasion, in particular, to sway people into buying something that works for them while also working for the salesperson's wallet. They become masters at reading people through understanding body language, developing a rapport with techniques taught through NLP, and persuading those around them into whatever serves everyone best.

Salespeople know they have to be convincing influencers to get the results they desire, and they do not balk away from the challenge. They instead learn to utilize dark psychology, whether intentionally or through experience, trial, and error, and those techniques are what ultimately make them particularly good salespeople. Those who understand the workings of the minds of those they must sell to are far more likely to be successful when attempting to close the deal.

Dark Psychology in Religion

Surprisingly enough, religion does utilize some of the principles found within dark psychology, namely those that appeal to emotions like fear. Through intense emotional influence, typically appealing to fear, the religion is able to keep people in line, which is ultimately what the fundamental purpose of religion was during the evolution of humankind. Religion gives those who practice whatever particular religion they are a part of a common purpose, a reason to work together for the same goal, which does influence them to behave in ways that are far more beneficial to everyone. With this sort of push toward commonality, people become better at living together, respecting each other, and helping each other.

Of course, that religion requires some way to keep people in line. For many, it is the threat of a negative outcome, whether that is a rejection from a particular afterlife, a denial of achieving nirvana and being reincarnated as a lesser being, or even just not being suddenly smitten where you stand. No matter the reason, each of those appeal to fear. When people are afraid, they are more open to suggestion, which allows for religious ideals to be pushed onto people during impressionable states, enabling for the perpetuation of religion as a whole.

Dark Psychology in Destructive Cults

This is an example of a more insidious use of dark psychology—you have not yet seen a glimpse into the darkness that these techniques can create, and this is one of them. In cults, particularly those that are more destructive, the group leader seeks to systematically brainwash the followers into complete obedience. Through a series of dark psychology tactics, people are systematically isolated, broken down, and sometimes even beaten into the fringes of society, where they are oftentimes forgotten, and taught to behave in ways that are solely beneficial for the cult. Personal needs do not need to be met within these cults, and selfishness is oftentimes punished.

Due to the charisma with which cult leaders draw in followers, the seduction tactics utilized, isolation, mind control, brainwashing, and more, people are transformed into obedient robots. Perhaps one of the most popular examples of this is the Peoples Temple of the Disciples of Christ cult in which Jim Jones, a cult leader, utilized several dark psychology tactics to build a cult. On November 18th, 1979, he convinced nearly 1000 of his followers to drink cyanide-laced drinks, and they all died. Those who were not convinced to drink were forced to drink it. While that is a rather extreme example, several cults to this day will intentionally subvert their followers in order to gain the ultimate control.

Dark Psychology in the Workplace

Not even the workplace is a safe place from dark psychology, even with the efforts of HR to make it such. Within workplaces, leaders and bosses can be seen utilizing various techniques within dark psychology, whether to persuade or encourage the employees or to intimidate them into believing that all will be lost if they do not give in to whatever it is that the bosses or people in charge seek. People at workplaces may be threatened with being fired if they cannot perform to the standards required, or they may find themselves under constant scrutiny. A wide range of different techniques can be used, and the end result is either the employee giving in or the employer firing him or her for not meeting standards. The entire purpose is because the employer or the company that is employing the employee, does not care about the individual—instead, the only thing that matters is the bottom line and whether the company is making money. If the individual responsible for the work is not making the company money, the individual is seen as a liability and is likely to be cut off for that reason alone. These employees are stuck between a rock and a hard place when faced with dark psychology in the workplace, as they can either take it and submit, or disagree and leave the job, which is not always a viable option. Someone with a family or who is reliant on his income and living paycheck to paycheck, like nearly 80% of US workers, will not be in a position to up and leave over a disagreement, and that alone can be enough to force them to accept whatever coercive threats and expectations the employer has demanded.

Chapter 3: Dark Psychology Users

With an understanding of the kinds of ways that dark psychology can be utilized, you are now free to begin understanding what those who utilize dark psychology look like. At a glance, there may be nothing of interest that differentiates the user from a normal person walking down the street, but the dark psychology user is so much more dangerous—they would be capable of absolutely destroying a person's life, unrooting everything if they felt the desire to do so.

Even though manipulators and dark psychology users come from every corner of the world, every culture, every class, every race, they all follow very similar, predictable patterns. They share certain traits that can be identified when you understand what to look for. These different traits come together to create dangerous individuals capable of anything and everything. These people, depending on how they utilize their skills and their propensities to target and victimize people based on their weaknesses or vulnerabilities, can either be incredibly functional, influential people, or they can become the worst of the worst, essentially a scourge on the human race, oftentimes compared to a cancer that would be better off removed than allowed to continue.

Traits of Dark Psychology Users

The dark psychology user typically follows these traits below. Of course, this is not a hard-and-fast rule, and some users are far more ethical, but those who are particularly dangerous will follow many of these traits with little deviation.

Egotistical

Perhaps one of the driving factors for many of the manipulators you are likely to face in your life is the egotistical nature many take on. So many of the manipulators you will encounter see themselves as the world's greatest gift to humankind, even though the vast majority of people would probably disagree when they got to know them.

These dark psychology users, particularly when dangerous, are so focused on themselves and what they want and need, that they do not care much about those around them. They are happy to sacrifice the wellbeing of one person to meet their needs because they see their own needs as far more important than the needs of those around them.

Lacking Empathy

Some dark psychology users, particularly those who are able to inflict the most harm, lack empathy. They may understand exactly what someone feels from a conceptual point, recognizing an emotion due to their skill at reading the emotions and body language of others, they do not really *feel* the other person's suffering in the way an empathetic individual would. This lends itself to the next trait, as those who do not empathize with their peers have far less incentive to stop harming those around them.

Disregard for Social Conventions or Morals

Many of the dark psychology users out to hurt others for their own selfish gains are entirely disengaged from social conventions. They do not care about laws, morality, or what society demands, seeing all of that as little more than societal constructs that are only necessary to control the people. They feel like there is no reason to control them, or they may simply just enjoy breaking the law and seeing what happens, and they act accordingly. They do what they want, even if it is illegal or immoral. The ends justify the means, and so long as the manipulator or user of dark psychology is satisfied, that is all that matters.

Entitled

Oftentimes, dark psychology users feel quite entitled. This is typically due to their own delusions of grandeur telling them just how important they are, feeding their egos and inflating them to disproportionate levels. Because of their overinflated egos, they believe that they are entitled to virtually anything just because they ask for it. If someone does not oblige nearly instantly, that person is seen as a threat, and that person is suddenly targeted for attack. The user will utilize anything within his arsenal to get the person to give him what he was expecting to receive because he is entitled to it, even if that means he has to coerce and force the other person into obedience.

Sadistic

Remember, most of those with dark personalities who also utilize dark psychology are predators at heart. They thrive off of the hunt and the defeat of their prey. They revel in what they are doing and will enjoy hurting those around them, especially if they are doing so because the other person did not do what they expected in the first place, seeing it as a way to sort of compensate for the disobedience that was shown in the first place.

Selfish

Along with entitled and egotistical, manipulators and other dark psychology users will see others around them as nothing more than stepping stones to get from point A to point B as quickly and efficiently as possible. They do not care about the interests of anything or anyone else, so long as their own wants and needs are met, and they will do anything to ensure their needs are met before anyone else's. They only act in ways that serve their own interests.

Impulsive

Much of the time, those who are dark psychology users are actually quite impulsive, even though the act of manipulating others requires immense amounts of patience and planning. They are impulsive in the sense that they are acting upon their whims. They want to ensure that they enjoy themselves, so if they impulsively decide that they will seduce a person they saw at a party, they will do so, by any means necessary.

Spiteful

Perhaps one of the most interesting traits of manipulators in general, is their propensity for spitefulness. They will do things just to spite those they have perceived as having wronged them in the past, even if their spiteful act will hurt them as well. They will simply take the damage to themselves and completely disregard it, so long as they are also hurting the other person. For example, a person who feels as though their ex-spouse has wronged them may decide to suddenly sue for everything; all custody, child support, and decision-making ability simply to spite the other person. They may have been the least involved parent ever, and continue to be entirely uninterested in parenting, but so long as the other person is hurting, it does not matter how miserable the individual is with the newfound responsibilities of children.

The Dark Triad

Perhaps the most well-known traits of those who utilize dark psychology is the collection known as the dark triad. This is a particularly insidious group, consisting of narcissism,

Machiavellianism, and psychopathy that combine to create a toxic monster that hardly deserves the name of a human. This personality type will be discussed in-depth in the next chapter.

Users of Dark Psychology

Now that you understand some of the traits typically associated with dark psychology, you can take a look at some of the most common uses of the manipulative techniques that will be discussed shortly. Remember, this is a generalization, and not every individual within each of these categories will behave in a way that is necessarily harmful, but they are likely to utilize at least some of the concepts found within dark psychology to their own advantage.

Salespeople

As already briefly touched upon, salespeople thrive off of manipulating or persuading others into buying from them. They directly benefit when they manage to upsell someone, and that alone can oftentimes be enough to sway them to do so, even if they would ordinarily believe that the acts of forcing the point or underhandedly persuading someone to do something would be considered wrong. Salespeople are stuck between two difficult choices—do not perform well and risk losing their jobs and livelihoods, or performing as well as possible and making some decisions that would largely be considered immoral by those around them. Unfortunately, when the ends justify the means, that means giving up some of your moral fortitude and doing things you wish you never had to do in the first place.

Politicians

Politicians have also briefly already been discussed—they are reliant on people being persuaded, or in some cases, manipulated or coerced, into doing what they want. They need people to want to vote for them if they want to get to positions of power. For that reason, they oftentimes will word things that are ambiguous, so people hear what they want to hear, and the politician does not have to lie about what was said. They do whatever is necessary to get the desired results.

Leaders

Like politicians, leaders must be able to captivate an audience and persuade them to obey or do as requested. Unlike politicians, however, good leaders emphasize ethical persuasion, always looking to do something in return, or ensuring that the needs of everyone are juggled. They know that remaining in power relies upon people legitimately liking them, and they seek to make that a reality.

Abusers

Now, this may be what you have read so far into the book to get to—abusers. Abusers love dark psychology. It gives them utter control over their target, and that utter control is absolutely *exhilarating*. They absolutely thrive off of being able to manipulate their targets simply for the fun of manipulating them with no real purpose necessary. This is not done for any reason other than personal enjoyment, and it is often quite insidious.

Chapter 4: The Dark Triad

Oftentimes, abusers fall within this category—the dark triad. The dreaded three personality types that together, combine to create a human storm capable of destroying lives so utterly that the individuals have little hope of reassembling them without intensive professional assistance. These personality types are dark—they do not care about people and encompass everything wrong and everything toxic about humanity. They are oftentimes monsters within human skin, staring out into the world and looking to wreak as much havoc as they can as quickly as possible. These three traits, Machiavellianism, narcissism, and psychopathy, are dangerous enough on their own, but when you find an individual who harnesses them all, be forewarned—you are better off leaving while you still can and escaping all of the nonsense altogether as quickly as possible.

Machiavellianism

If you had to simplify Machiavellianism into the shortest possible phrase, it would be one that you have already read several times throughout this book— "The ends justify the means." This phrase, though never directly stated by Niccolo Machiavelli, an Italian politician and philosopher from the 1500s, came from the text he wrote in *The Prince* in 1513—he informed the prince that was being instructed within the document to present himself in one way, honest and benevolent, even though he was ready to behave as harshly as necessary because everyone can see a person, but very few people will ever actually get close enough to realize the truth. The message is essentially summed up by saying that the ends justify the means, meaning that it was acceptable to lie because it made the prince more well-liked, and a well-liked leader is far more likely to be a successful leader that is able to maintain power.

Drawing from that principle, Machiavellian people are adept at appearing the way those around them wish to see them. They will absolutely say whatever those around them want to hear because they know that it is unlikely that those around them will ever know the truth, and telling them what they want to hear makes them happier and gets the Machiavellian person what he or she wants. The end, then, getting the desired result, justifies the means of lying, even though lying is typically considered morally wrong and reprehensible.

This personality type is quite insidious—you never know whether what you are seeing is what you are actually getting. The Machiavellian individual is deceitful, and a master at deceiving people around him or her. They will only tell the truth if it is beneficial to them or is actually the most desired result, which it usually is not. They assume that it is more important to seem desirable and to make good connections than it is to develop actual proper relationships with people, but when you see people as nothing more than a means to an end, you are not likely to ever want to develop a relationship with others. When people are nothing but means, they have been dehumanized, turned into nothing but tools to be utilized to get what you want in any way possible simply because you want that result. Ultimately, despite the immorality of the behavior, you will do whatever it is that you must in order to get the result you want simply because it will get you what you want and that is all you really care about at the end of the day.

These people should never be trusted—they always have an ulterior motive, no matter how truthful they may seem in the moment. There is always something motivating them to behave in certain ways, whether it is innocent or not is what is up for debate. You are better off avoiding and not trusting this person, whenever possible.

Narcissism

The next of the dark triad is the narcissist—those with narcissism are individuals that are suffering from a narcissistic personality disorder. This is characterized when an individual presents with a grandiose sense of self, meaning he is quite egotistical and believes that he is far superior than he actually is, a pervasive lack of empathy, and an excessive need for admiration and attention. The narcissist thrives off of getting his or her sense of self-justified through actions such as praise or admiration—they only see themselves as worthwhile if others around see them as worthwhile first. They want to be recognized as worthy and will do whatever it takes to get that.

This means that narcissists are oftentimes willing to lie about who they are or what they like—they have no true sense of self beyond someone that desperately seeks the approval and admiration of others, no matter what the cost, and is willing to do whatever it takes to get it, even if that means lying about who they are.

The narcissist typically creates an alter ego of sorts, a persona that he presents to the world that is everything he wishes he was—charismatic, powerful, influential, and well-liked. He then utilizes several dark psychology manipulation techniques in order to keep people under the spell he seeks to create. He creates a sense of self and then constantly plays mind games and manipulates those around him. Only those who get close enough to him to be ensnared in his web of lies beyond hope of getting out ever see his true self—the malicious individual that lies beneath the persona, lurking for the first possible chance to lash out at those around him.

After ensnaring a victim within his trap, he will systematically manipulate the other person, conditioning them into doing whatever the narcissist desires. Over time, he is able to mold his victim into the perfect source of constant admiration; something referred to as his narcissistic supply. He will then constantly utilize manipulation and mind control techniques to keep his new toy under his thumb for as long as possible, attempting to systematically break down his victim by any means necessary.

Psychopathy

Psychopaths suffer from their own personality disorders in which they are often characterized through a series of persistent antisocial actions. They almost always lack any real sense of empathy—the innate human ability to connect emotionally with others at any meaningful level. This lack of empathy makes them incredibly dangerous. Without empathy, which is sort of a built-in red flag system that lets us understand when something is wrong with those around us, particularly in regards to our own behaviors to others, the psychopath has no real fail-safe to his or her behaviors—he will continue to push and push, even with the most aggressive behaviors, simply because he does not feel any need to stop. For those who do feel empathy, the pain they, themselves, feel as they harm someone else, is usually enough to make them stop. The pain and guilt become overwhelming, and they stop before making it worse. The psychopath, however, does not feel that.

Beyond the lack of empathy and therefore remorse, typically, psychopaths also exhibit disinhibited behaviors—in simpler words, they are impulsive. A thought will pop into their mind with some random impulse, such as stealing a purse from someone or deciding to hurt another person, and they are far more likely to act upon it simply because they like to act upon their impulses.

Psychopaths are frequently also bold—they do not really fear anything they are approached with. Consequences are not intimidating. People are not intimidating. Even dying or being harmed is not intimidating to the psychopath. The psychopath is incredibly tolerant of danger, and is frequently noticed to have high levels of confidence and assertiveness, despite the fact that he is not likely to want to do anything meaningful with that confidence—he sees no point in engaging in social conventions.

The Dark Triad

With those three personality types now described in an easy-to-understand manner, you may now be wondering what happens when the three are combined. The results are an aggressive, toxic individual who does not care to act in a normal manner. They are fantastic at exploitation, lacking the empathy necessary to impede such negative, harmful behavior, and having the right amount of lack of impulse control to encourage it. They manipulate, they hurt, they steal, and they lie. They are callous, meaning they do not care about the feelings of others, and, in fact, revel in seeing people hurt, angry, or sad. Research has actually shown that people with the dark triad personality type all enjoyed seeing people with negative expressions on their faces.

Ultimately, those possessing the dark triad are not forces to be reckoned with—they will do anything that will hurt you if you wrong them, and they do not care enough about social conventions to be held back from seriously harming you.

Chapter 5: Reading Micro-Expressions and Body Language

With the nitty-gritty details about dark psychology, manipulators, and the dark triad out of the way, it is time to get to some skills you will be able to utilize later. The first and most important skill that will be at the foundation of everything, is the ability to read and recognize the feelings and general comfort of those around you. This chapter will provide you with a crash-course of recognizing the body language of others. It will be a lot of information all at once, so do not be afraid of taking this section in smaller chunks, working on small amounts of the body language at one time and mastering the identifying of that particular language before moving on to more.

Expressions

Body language is surprisingly universal—while several cultures will have their own unique gestures and readings of gestures, there are several types of body language that mean the same things across cultures and oceans. This may be, in part, due to the fact that humans have seven basic emotions that are believed to be at the root of all feelings that can be felt. These seven emotions are perhaps the most simplified versions of what is being felt, each encompassing a wide range of different emotions that can be felt by humans. Each of the emotions that will be listed here will describe facial expressions associated with them, with the next section afterward discussing more specific details about what certain stances may mean.

Happiness

Happiness is often characterized by two identifying factors on the face—the eyes should be crinkled, with a wrinkle at the corners that is next to impossible to fake, and by a smile, either wide or small.

Sadness

Sadness is characterized, namely by drawing eyebrows together. They are pulled together, with the innermost corners shifting upwards and causing wrinkles in between them. Along with these distinctive eyebrows, which are incredibly difficult to replicate without genuine feeling, oftentimes, the mouth is pulled downward into a frown with the bottom lip pouting outward.

Fear/Anxiety

In response to anxiety or fear, people typically raise their eyebrows, with the arch relatively straight. The forehead will show wrinkles between the brows as well. The eyes are usually widened, with the whites of the eyes being visible above the iris, and the pupils are usually dilated as well. This dilation of pupils is impossible to mimic, occurring entirely unconsciously. Oftentimes, the mouth is open as well, with the lips slightly parted and tensed.

Contempt

In contempt, the expression is actually almost entirely neutral. The only exception is a slight raise of one corner of the mouth for a moment during a hard stare, as if flashing a smirk.

Disgust

When someone feels disgusted, they look at it with lowered brows and pinched, raised eyelids. Usually, the nose wrinkles backward with the nostrils flared out, and the upper lip rises up, flashing teeth. This essentially shields the sensitive parts of the body—the eyes and nose are protected from whatever disgusting thing has caused such a strong reaction.

Anger

Anger typically involves lowered brows that hood the eyes, their brows coming together in the middle and creating a wrinkled forehead. Their eyes are usually staring without blinking in a harsh, hostile glare, and lips are tense.

Surprise

Surprise is usually noticeable by someone exhibiting raised eyebrows, with the arch nice and rounded. The upper part of the forehead is usually wrinkled as well, and the eyes are wide, with the whites being visible around the entire iris. The mouth may also be hung loosely open.

Facial Body Language

Beyond those most common emotional expressions, it is important to understand whether individual movements of the face are good or bad, as well as what they are implying. Take a look at the eyebrows, eyes, and mouth, and learn the most telling positions and movements they take unconsciously. Keep in mind, however, that when people are trying to hide deceit, they often control their face. It is not always the most reliable source of expressions or honesty, although it can be useful.

Eyebrows

- **Lowering the brows:** When you encounter someone with lowered brows, oftentimes, they are showing that what they want more than anything else is to not be engaged in whatever is happening. Whether angry, stuck in a confrontation, or disgusted, the connotation is almost always negative. It is also a telltale sign of deceit, especially when the person lowers their head in conjunction with lowering their brows.

- **Raising the brows:** Raising brows, on the other hand, shows increased attention or a sort of emphasis. It is seen in surprise when something suddenly and unexpectedly draws one's attention, and it can also be seen in people who are showing attraction in someone else.

- **One brow raised:** When one brow is raised, it usually shows disbelief or dubiousness at what was just said. It almost always brings along a connotation of not believing whatever was just said, or that someone disagrees with you. A quick twitch of one brow can also be seen in contempt sometimes.

- **Knitting brows together:** When the brows come together, they also create creases between them. It can be seen in negative, stressed emotions such as sadness, worry, and confusion.

- **Lowering the middle of the brows:** Typically, lowering the middle of the brows, creating a straight line rather than any real arch implies a frustration or anger being felt.

- **Raising the middle of the brows:** When the middle of the brows are raised, on the other hand, it usually shows either surprise, fear, or even relief. Because of the contradictory nature of some of the meanings to this expression, you should take it in conjunction with some other body language as well to be sure of the meaning.

Eyes

The eyes can communicate more than people would be likely to expect—after all, all they do is roll around to direct gaze, right?

Wrong.

They are also used to make and hold eye contact, the pupils can dilate and constrict, and even the frequency at which you blink can be telling of what is happening in your mind at any given moment.

- **Direction of gaze:** Interestingly enough, even the direction you look can be telling as to what is happening within your mind. When you look at someone or something, it is because you are interested in it. Especially if you notice that someone's gaze is repeatedly returning to the same thing over and over again, you have a likely sign that they are interested in something that is not you or your conversation. For example, looking constantly at another person implies that the individual would rather go speak to that other person, or looking at a drink implies that the person wants it. This can even go one step further—the direction your eyes turn when asked a question while you think can also decipher whether you are truthful. When you look to the left, you are utilizing the parts of your brain that recall memories. When you look to the right, you utilize the part of your brain used for creation and fiction, implying the creation of lies. When you look down, however, you appear to be shameful, and people often assume you are lying.

- **Intensity of gaze:** Have you noticed how some people can just stare you down with an unwavering gaze, but it makes you uncomfortable? Or how others may struggle to make eye contact with you at all, constantly looking away from you instead? The intensity of the gaze and how often you spend making eye contact tells how comfortable you are. The most natural, comfortable eye contact that implies that you are welcome and encouraged to continue speaking involves occasional glances away from the eyes but returning to continue eye contact shortly after. Too much eye contact is aggressive, confrontational, and unnerving. Too little shows shame, fear, or deception.

- **Frequency of blinking:** Along with the intensity of your gaze, people tend to look at how often you blink when you are making eye contact. Those who do not blink when making eye contact come across as far more aggressive than those who blink at a normal rate. Blinking too much, however, implies that you are flustered or stressed out. The rate of blinking can also allow you to identify when someone is lying—during the process of lying, oftentimes individuals do not blink at all while telling a lie, but immediately afterward, blink more often than usual.

- **Pupil dilation:** Pupil dilation is also important to understand, even though in most instances, you are not likely to be close enough to recognize the tiny shifts in levels. However, pupil dilations are impossible to fake, making them incredibly reliable. Typically, the pupils will dilate in response to something attractive, something surprising, something frightening, or when someone is lost in intensive thought—the more dilated the pupil, the more intense the thought.

Mouth

The mouth also can provide some pretty useful information if you direct your attention to it, and not just through verbal communication—the way that the mouth moves, whether open or shut, tense or relaxed, or even with the other person touching their mouth, can tell more of the story than the words ever will.

- **Lips are relaxed:** When the lips are relaxed, the person is usually relaxed. They are likely confident, comfortable, and in control of the situation without any worry or stress.

- **Lips are parted:** Usually, when the lips are parted, the individual is flirting with the other person. However, it is also used when one person is trying to get the attention of another, typically in the context of wanting the person to stop talking so they can speak as well.

- **Teeth are bared:** When someone bares their teeth, they are either smiling, which is positive, or snarling, which shows that the other person is feeling intense anger or aggression.

- **Lips are twitching:** When the lips are twitching, particularly on one side, it shows either contempt or an attempt to hide one's feelings. Usually, the twitch was the uncontrollable impulse to do something, but the person overrode that impulse, leaving behind only a nearly imperceptible twitch of the lip in its wake.

- **Touching the mouth or biting the fingers:** When someone is touching their mouth or biting their fingers, they are either under stress and attempting to self-soothe, or they are hiding something from you.

- **Biting the cheek or the lip:** Oftentimes, biting the cheek or lip also implies that the other person is nervous, afraid, unsure how to react, or is attempting to hold back a true reaction.

Body Language

Beyond facial features, the body itself is just as expressive. The way the body moves can tell you a surprising amount of details about what is happening within the other person's mind, ranging from feeling entirely uncomfortable with an interaction, to feeling confident, in control, and powerful. Keep in mind that some people may express themselves in different ways and that this suggestion should be approached as a guide and not a guarantee to help you identify any emotions in anyone else.

Head

The first part of the body you will learn about will be the head. The head, beyond expressions and facial features, can be moved in a wide variety of ways that can also help provide insight into the mind of another.

- **Tilt:** People naturally direct their head toward those they feel a rapport, or connection, with. Even when that person is not necessarily talking in a group, people will unconsciously tilt their heads toward the leader of the group. It can also tilt toward someone that they feel a connection with. Conversely, tilting the head back, away from someone, implies distrust, suspicion, or being unsure in general. By tilting the head to the side, an individual encourages the other person to continue speaking.

- **Nod:** When someone nods, it is usually a sign of affirmation, confirming the agreement, or confirming that the individual is listening. When someone nods quicker, it means they are growing impatient and want to disengage, but feel too polite to do so. When the nodding is slower and more thoughtful, it implies that the other person is still actively listening and engaged in the conversation.

- **Watch the chin:** The chin, like the tilt of the head, can show a lot. When the chin is raised upwards, the neck is exposed. This is a sign of arrogance—it is essentially daring the other person to even try touching them or hurting them. When it is tucked downward, shielding the neck, however, it shows a level of insecurity.

Arms/shoulders

The way the arms are held can also be incredibly revealing. Take a look at some of the most common ways that arms are held and what they mean:

- **Arms pulled backward:** When the arms are drawn backward, it is usually because the individual feels uncomfortable or defensive. In drawing backward, they are able to make their arms less available to grab—as the shoulders move away, they are less readily available during an attack.

- **Arms expanded:** The arms can be expanded outward, relaxed at the shoulders and allowed to hang naturally. This is a sign of openness and comfort, implying that the other person is comfortable with what is happening at the moment.

- **Arms drawn inward:** Conversely to expanding the arms, when the arms are pulled inward, the individual is seen as making him or herself smaller and therefore less of a target. It implies insecurity or discomfort.

- **Arms entirely still:** When the arms are entirely still at the sides, they typically look quite unnatural, and for a good reason—usually the other person is trying to control their arms to avoid exposing any body language that could be taken advantage of later. This can go one step further as well, with one arm crossing the body so one hand can hold the other arm still as if physically restraining it. This is a tell for lying as well, as the individual is literally holding him or herself back.

- **Arms crossed:** Arms crossed is often seen as the ultimate form of defensiveness—usually the individual feels incredibly uncomfortable with whatever is happening and is literally shielding his vulnerable chest—protecting the vital organs within his ribcage from attack.

- **Arms raised upwards:** Sometimes, arms are thrown upwards, above the shoulder lines. Usually, this is in some sort of emphasis—either in joy, surprise, or even confusion.

Hands

Like the arms, the hands are also incredibly expressive. Because they can be moved in so many different ways, they can be used to show a wide range of different feelings and mental states.

- **Hands-on hips:** Hands on the hips may often come across as aggressive or intimidating, but it is actually meant to be a power pose—it instills confidence and implies a readiness to act.

- **Palms upward:** When palms are turned upwards, it typically implies someone is trying to be seen as trustworthy, worth listening to, and is speaking earnestly.

- **Palms downward:** When the palms are downwards, however, it conveys dominance and control—this is often seen in politics. People or leaders will put their hands outward to signify that they have control of the situation. They may also punctuate their words with a few chopping motions downwards, essentially forcing the point they are trying to get across.

- **Hands behind back:** Hand behind the back can happen in several different ways—the hands can be relaxed, with one hand resting in the palm of the other, or it could involve one hand holding onto the wrist or arm of the other. When the hands are resting together, it implies dominance, control, and authority. It is calm and collected. When the hand is gripping the other hand, however, it implies that the other person is attempting to control himself. The higher the handgrips, the more out of control that person feels in that particular moment.

- **Hands in pockets:** Oftentimes, this is seen as deceptive, or maybe done out of anxiety as well.

- **Steepling:** Steepling involves the palms facing each other but never touching, and the fingertips of both hands resting against each other. When this happens, the other person is showing that they are confident, in control, and that they are powerful.

- **Clenched fists:** When fists are clenched, usually the other person is attempting to exert control over themselves—they may feel stressed or out of control and be trying to get it back. They may also be feeling extreme anger, frustration, or aggression.

- **Rubbing hands together:** When the hands rub together, a person is signifying that he or she is anticipating something and is excited about whatever will come next.

- **Pointing:** Pointing is often considered quite aggressive and dominant, much like a parent scolding his or her children. It can be accentuated by someone turning the point into a jab.

- **Hands-on heart:** When someone places a hand or hands on the heart, they are typically attempting to show that they are speaking from the heart. Of course, this is incredibly easy to falsify, so keep in mind that the other person may not be being as honest as they are attempting to imply.

- **Tapping fingers:** When the person is tapping their fingers along their arm, desk, or any other surface, the other person is trying to signal that they are impatient and would like the conversation or interaction to wrap up as quickly as possible.

Legs/feet

The last part of the body you will look at is the legs, and the feet attached to them. These parts of the body are typically forgotten by those who are attempting to disguise their body language, and because of that, it is a great baseline to identify true intentions. The mouth may lie, but the feet tell the truth. The next time you are talking to someone and are unsure about what the other person is thinking at the moment, try looking at their feet—you will likely get some valuable information.

- **Crossed legs:** This can show dominance, so long as you do it with an ankle over a knee. Of course, that is largely a male position. When the legs are crossed over the knees, particularly with women, it shows flirtation. When the legs are crossed at the ankles, it shows that you are anxious, afraid, or uncertain.

- **Sitting with legs spread:** This shows that you are marking an area as your own—you are showing that you are dominant over it and not afraid to fight someone for it.

- **Pointing feet toward the speaker:** When the feet are pointing toward the speaker, it is a good sign that the listeners are incredibly engaged in the conversation. They may be interested in the speaker as a person, or in whatever is being said. Regardless, this is a good sign, and the conversation is encouraged to continue.

- **Pointing feet away from the speaker:** When you notice that the other person is pointing their feet away, however, there is a high likelihood that the other person is disengaged from the speaker. They may be interested in something else more, such as leaving or going to speak to someone else. Check to see where the person's feet are pointing if you want to understand what it is that they want at that moment.

- **Toes pointed up:** When toes point upwards as if the person has shifted their stance slightly so their heel is rolled back and toes go upward, the person is likely relaxed and enjoying any interaction that is happening at that moment. Check to see if they are showing other signs of relaxation as well—you'll likely find a smile and relaxed arms.

- **Bouncing on feet:** Much like a child literally jumping in the air in joy or excitement, adults will also bounce a bit—usually, they tone down the behavior, so they are not seen as childish, but you can notice a shift in their feet.

- **Tapping feet:** If the other person is tapping their feet, but there is no music playing, chances are the other person is not interested in what is happening. It can show signs of anxiety, impatience, or disinterest and wanting to leave.

Proxemics

While proxemics may have a fancy name, it is actually quite simple. It refers to the distance between yourself and someone else. It is also incredibly telling in terms of the relationship or rapport between the two people you are observing.

Close

When two people are sitting or standing close together, it typically implies they have a good relationship. The closer the two are to each other physically, the more intimate or close the relationship is. For example, if you see a married couple standing together, you will likely notice them standing so closely that they are touching each other without trying to. Standing that close to a stranger or an enemy would send huge red flags to the other person, and they would likely back off, attempting to put distance between the two of you. You can also use this during interviews or other social interactions to get a feel for what is happening. If the other person steps closer to you, they are likely enjoying what you are saying or who you are. You can also test how they feel about you by slowly closing the gap between yourself and the other person—if they pull back when you shift toward them, then they may not be interested in you, or at least, they do not want a closer relationship.

Far

Conversely, when the other person intentionally places some distance between himself or herself and you, shifting away whenever you move closer or leaning away from you when you lean inward, they want distance. They may want the interaction itself to end, or they may be interested in you but not yet comfortable with who you are as a person. Remember, unless you want to come across as intimidating, frustrating, aggressive, or dominant, do not repeatedly attempt to close the gap if the other person is intentionally leaving a gap and actively attempting to maintain it.

Chapter 6: Covert Emotional Manipulation

Covert emotional manipulation is something most people wish they never would become involved with, but by the time they realize they may be getting manipulated, the damage has already been done. It involves one person intentionally, systematically, and covertly removing as much power as possible from another person, instead of replacing it with control. The victim never knows it is happening, and the manipulator essentially gains near-total control over the other person. When it is finally discovered, the individual who is being controlled realizes that he or she is lost—not realizing what has happened, confused about how their entire life has spiraled out of their own control and feeling as though they are stuck.

What is Covert Emotional Manipulation?

Covert emotional manipulation has three key parts:

- Covert

- Emotional

- Manipulation

Understanding all three of these parts will be necessary if you want to understand what happens within this type of manipulation. Before delving into how it is done or what techniques manipulators tend to prefer, you will first define all three of these key parts.

Covert, at its simplest, means secret. It refers to how secretive the entire process is—the manipulator is able to install all of the strings necessary without detection, utilizing all sorts of methods that employ plausible deniability. This means that they do things that are intentionally ambiguous—they may be hurtful things, but when the victim calls the individual out on being so hurtful, the manipulator denies everything, claiming that the victim is far too sensitive about such things and needs to learn to relax a little.

Emotional means that it will employ tactics whose success will hinge upon the ability to successfully use emotions. The emotions of choice that manipulators usually go for are fear and sadness, as both of these enable the manipulator to better control the victim. Essentially, the manipulator will cause the feeling of one of these emotions to use as a foundation for whatever behavior he may be attempting to manipulate or coerce out of the victim.

Manipulation means that the manipulator is swaying the victim into doing something. The actions at that point are not done of the victim's volition—there was some sort of coercion or force that occurred, whether through threats, fear, or anything else, and that allows for the manipulator to retain control.

Essentially, with covert emotional manipulation, the manipulator is the puppet-master, creating all sorts of invisible strings in the victim behind the scenes in ways that go entirely undetected. These strings allow for the emotional manipulation of the other person, which can then be used to the manipulator's advantage as they extort, coerce, and force the victim into behaving to avoid intense emotional distress.

How to Use Covert Emotional Manipulation

When you want to use covert emotional manipulation, you must follow two major steps once your target has been primed and is open and receptive to these types of behaviors. You must first create emotions into the target, and then you must be able to exploit those emotions. If you can create and exploit the right emotions within someone, you can sway their behaviors into whatever results you hope to achieve. Typically, the easiest emotions to utilize for this process are fear, anxiety, or sadness. Guilt also works quite well as well—very little is as motivating as some intense guilt.

Emotions for Manipulating

- **Fear:** When you feel fear or anxiety, you are typically expecting something negative to happen. Usually, you are tensed up, afraid, and waiting for the other shoe to drop, so whatever negative consequence or action that you are anticipating can happen. Usually, this is in response to some sort of threat or danger—you are certain you will be harmed if you are not careful. That fear or anxiety usually plays an important role in your emotional regulation and your survival—when you are afraid, you go into fight or flight response, meaning your body prepares to either fight back or run away. Blood is redirected away from unimportant areas, such as the extremities, and from the higher processing areas in the brain. This, unfortunately, means that your higher-level thinking is impaired when you are afraid, and has the effect of leaving you far more susceptible to being convinced or swayed into doing something that you would not normally entertain. You act in fear, just wanting to make the fear or anxiety go away so you can return to your baseline feelings of calmness or happiness.

- **Sadness:** When you are sad, usually something bad has happened, and you are mourning or grieving something. You feel a profound loss of something and that hole that whatever it is you are missing hurts. In fact, sadness is a huge motivator for people—it encourages people to avoid repeating mistakes out of fear of losing something else. When you are sad, your mind and body are essentially telling you to not repeat whatever had just happened because it was bad. Of course, when people are sad, their rational minds are not working entirely—those who make decisions when sad are far more likely to be swayed by someone else. If the manipulator can get their target to fall into sadness, the target is more likely to go along with anything the manipulator says, simply wanting to be freed of the sadness that is overwhelming him or her.

- **Guilt:** Guilt is what we feel when we fail to complete an obligation. Ultimately, we feel obligations to those we love and trust the most—it is a sort of way that we ensure that everyone we care about survives. We feel obligated to take care of our children, and that drives most mothers to get out of bed at 3 am when they hear their babies crying for milk, or when the kids are up at 5:30 on the dot, even on Saturday, begging for breakfast. Obligation is what makes you do selfless things for those you love. When you fail to meet those obligations, however, you feel guilt. That guilt lets you know that you failed, and those negative feelings are meant to make you not repeat that mistake again. After all, not meeting obligations could mean the difference between life and death in some situations, and the biological imperative wants you and those you share genes with to survive. When you feel guilty, you are likely to do whatever you can in order to get out from underneath it.

Creating Emotions

With your understanding of the easiest emotions to manipulate, you now need to take a look at how to instill those emotions in someone else. When you understand how to create an emotion within someone else with very little effort, you are able to make sure you can always control them. The easiest way to create an emotion in someone is to recognize that emotions are motivators—if you can figure out the right trigger, you can create the emotion.

For example, if you need to make the person you are trying to control feel guilty in order to get them to do something for you, you would first ask them. When they say no, the trick here is to sigh, pretend to sadly accept the results while referencing how you know how much of a hassle what you are asking about is and that you remember how difficult it was when you did it for the other person. You are likely to hit some guilt buttons in response, triggering the feelings of guilt and therefore making it more likely to get what you want.

On the other hand, if you wanted to create sadness, you could tell a story that you know has a sad result just to get the other person into the right frame of mind. For example, if you know the target has children, referring to children dying or getting hurt could get the other person into a sad mindset pretty quickly. This particular emotion is useful when attempting to raise money—appeal to the saddest part of the organization, showing pictures of the starving children that look like they are on the brink of death or the dogs with the sad eyes. The feelings will follow afterward.

Exploiting Emotions

With the feelings created, it is game time. You can finally begin to exploit them. If you really wanted to go to that game, but your spouse told you no, it is time to pull out the guilt cards. If you are trying to pass a sale on a certain car, appeal to safety features in the model you are pushing. While anger is not typically a very good one to intentionally create because those who are angry are typically less receptive to suggestions, it can have its uses, and if you notice that someone is angry, redirect that anger to someone or something else that will aid you in whatever it is you want.

Why Use Covert Emotional Manipulation?

Ultimately, there are several reasons for using covert emotional manipulation, and all of them are quite underhanded. Despite that, you may find something on this list that actually helps you somehow.

Sales

In sales, this can actually be a fantastic skill to utilize, so long as you make it a point to ensure you are selling what is beneficial to the clients that approach you and you do not sell items that have no use to the other person just to get the bonus or sales credit. Utilizing emotional manipulation can actually be quite useful if you believe the other person is making a bad decision and would be better served with some other purchase instead.

Advertising

Similar to sales, covert emotional manipulation runs rampant throughout various forms of advertising. Everything from the way the pages are formatted to what kinds of pictures are used, are put together in order to create an immersive experience, appealing to whatever emotions will best sell the product that is being advertised.

Politics

Politicians frequently can use this in order to distract from bigger issues at hand and to gain favor in crowds that might not have been so open without it. For example, they may be able to recognize ways that one group could be swayed, such as appealing to conservative older people with vows of sharing religion and being interested in maintaining said religion, or in siding with younger people through discussing ways to better the economy and protect those who are struggling.

Getting What You Want

One of the most common ways that covert emotional manipulation is used, however, is to get what you want. Typically, abusers will utilize it this way, seeking to install all sorts of emotional triggers in their victims and then pulling them whenever they see it necessary to get the right results.

Chapter 7: Covert Emotional Manipulation Tactics

Now that you have developed a solid understanding of what covert emotional manipulation requires to be effective, as well as how the process works, you are ready to begin looking at several different tactics that are regularly used in a wide range of situations. Remember, not all of these will be appropriate to use in professional settings, such as in sales or in politics, but they are effective techniques.

As you read through each of these, you will see how each seeks to cause an emotion and then subsequently take advantage of it shortly after. During this cycle, people are able to essentially control the emotional reactions of those around them. They are able to cause people to feel all sorts of things, through a wide range of skills, and utilize those skills to the fullest potential they have.

Love Bombing and Rejection

Perhaps one of the simplest tactics used, but still incredibly effective, is the love bomb and rejection cycle. With this technique, you essentially are repeatedly love bombing to addict the other person to you before suddenly withdrawing affection altogether.

Love bombing refers to the tactic of showering someone in all sorts of lavish, meaningful affection, praise, and reinforcements. The purpose of this is to flood the body with all sorts of positive hormones, essentially mimicking the act of falling in love. As you constantly love on someone else, you are rapidly flooding their body with good hormones. As you do this, you are tricking them. Everyone feels good when they are showered with praise, after all—that praise can be incredibly reinforcing. The more the target feels the praise, the love, and the affection, the more thoroughly he or she will be addicted.

Frequently, manipulators will use this carefully, appealing to everyone's inherent desire to be loved and wanted. They will very carefully identify a target, choosing someone who they believe will be receptive to suck manipulation and act quickly. These people are suddenly pushing a whirlwind romance, driving the relationship forward as they do so. They encourage the other person to say that they love the manipulator as quickly as possible. They want the other person to be entirely and utterly intoxicated by the manipulator's very presence, and constant praise and reinforcement is the way to do so. Through conditioning, the target associates the positive feelings created by the praise and reinforcement with the individual, even though the individual may be less than deserving of such association.

When the target is thoroughly ensnared into the manipulator's trap, the target's threshold for dealing with unwarranted or unacceptable behavior is elevated—because the target feels as though he or she loves the manipulator, he or she is willing to accept far more from the manipulator than someone who was not essentially addicted to the person's very presence.

This is then tested in the rejection stage. Here, the manipulator will intentionally knock the target off of the elevated pedestal onto which he or she worked so hard to place the individual. Suddenly, the manipulator withdraws all sorts of affection, replacing it with scorn or disdain, and the target is suddenly shocked. Like a drug addict, desperate to score as soon as possible in any way possible, the target will do nearly anything necessary to get back into the good graces of the manipulator, craving those scraps of attention and affection and all the good feelings those scraps will bring.

This cycle is repeated again and again, essentially keeping the individual target ensnared in a never-ending cycle. The victim feels affection and wanted for a short period, only to be sent crashing back down through rejection and desperately attempting to climb back up the ranks.

Reinforcement and Repetition

Something that this book has not yet touched upon is the idea that reinforcing an idea several times is enough to instill that belief into someone else as well. Through repeatedly mentioning something, that something becomes believed. This concept can be incredibly useful in a wide range of situations, but perhaps the most profound is the idea that a completely false piece of information can be installed. The key here is to choose out a method that will best benefit the manipulator.

For example, imagine that you are in a relatively new relationship with a woman. You have gone through the love-bombing stages and are now interested in pushing the possibilities a bit further. You decide to convince the victim of something now. In thinking, you realize that perhaps the best concept that would serve you well is that the other person should feel lucky to have you.

With that in mind, you repeatedly begin dropping hints around the victim. You mention how lucky the victim is to have such a loving, caring partner like yourself. Even if you are doing something entirely mundane and expected that does not deserve praise, such as taking out the garbage unprompted, you mention how lucky your victim is to have someone like you that cares enough to help without being told to do so.

A little later in the day, you may decide to bring your victim a glass of water while she checks emails on her computer. She thanks you and again, you take the chance to add in a quick reference to how lucky she is to have you.

After several instances of you naturally dropping such hints, you will be rewarded with the moment of truth—you will do something entirely unordinary and expected, and she will thank you profusely and reiterate just how happy she feels to have you as a partner. This is how you know you did it right.

Now, praise that thought process. Shower her with love and affection after she has said it, and she is going to have that concept reinforced in her mind. Unconsciously, she will develop a connection between that thought and good feelings, and she will continue to entertain it.

With the thought installed, you are able to use it whenever necessary. You can threaten to withhold affection or break up if she does not do what you ask. If she argues back about something, you can remind her just how lucky she is and that if she isn't careful, she will lose a really good thing. As you will soon discover, you are appealing to one of the principles of persuasion here—reiterating how much she stands to lose if she does not get in line, and she is likely to give in out of fear of losing what she now believes is the greatest thing that has ever happened to her thanks to your very own manipulation tactics. You inflate the value of the relationship and then utilize the fear of losing that relationship to pull strings and keep the victim in line and obedient.

Gaslighting

Gaslighting is perhaps the most insidious of the methods on this list. When you are gaslighting someone, you are literally telling them that whatever they are saying or perceiving about your surroundings are entirely false. Through several steps, you will systematically erode the perception of reality the individual target possesses. You will make them afraid that they cannot trust their own perception of the world around them, no matter how accurate their perceptions may be, and you will use it to your advantage.

You will start out by denying small details about things—details that, while on their own, would be innocuous white lies, such as saying you bought that really good pizza at store A, not store B when in reality it came from store B. There may be no reason to lie about where something came from, or where you found something, but you want to plant the inkling of the idea that the individual could actually be unable to perceive reality accurately.

After several reiterations of tiny details being tweaked, you can move up in intensity—you can change the details of something your victim has perceived or found. When she walks into a room to tell you that she will be paying a certain bill that afternoon, for example, you could tell her she had already paid it the other day. Of course, keep in mind that you should not be ruining anyone else's credit, so you should probably make sure that bill gets paid anyway. Laugh off her forgetting about the bill, pointing out just how forgetful she has been in recent days without making a big deal about it.

Next, you move to something a little bigger—you can deny something you have said during a conversation in order to convince her that she is making things up. It could be a simple detail, or it could be you denying that something major was said, even if you did say whatever it was. As you slowly ramp up the intensity of how much you are willing to deny or fabricate, you are then able to really convince her that she cannot trust her own perceptions. You eventually get to the point where you can tell her all sorts of random lies and have her believe them, such as that no one will believe her if she reaches out for help to leave the relationship, or that she will never find anyone who will love her in the future.

The end result here is someone who is complacent and obedient, fearing that her own perceptions are inherently flawed and deciding instead to rely on the perceptions of those around her. She will defer to the manipulator to make decisions for her first and foremost but will accept the decisions of others around her as well as proper substitutes for her own judgment. When she cannot trust herself, she will feel the need to rely on others to guide her way instead, creating someone you can utterly control.

FOG

FOG is an acronym, standing for fear, obligation, and guilt. We have already touched upon some of these concepts at this point, but it is time to reiterate them—with this concept, you are appealing to either fear, obligation, or guilt in order to pressure someone into helping you. Each of these three points can be incredibly useful in manipulating others, as each is a major motivator.

This is perhaps one of the hardest methods of manipulation to maintain as it requires nearly constant leverage above the other person and something that can always be utilized. For family members, people often appeal to obligation, but other people can find other ways to instill fear within someone to keep them in line.

When you want to instill fear, you need to have some sort of power. It could be the threat of a spouse removing children if you dare attempt a divorce, and barring you from future access to those children, or it could be the idea that if you do not give someone the money they are asking for, then their own family will be utterly ruined, or they will tell all sorts of deep secrets to the world. Ultimately, there must be something that is feared in order for the manipulator to appeal to fear. If you can identify what someone's fear is, you can extort it here.

The next option is obligation—this has already been touched upon. Obligation is the feeling of loyalty that motivates humans to take care of those close to them. If you like someone, you likely feel some sense of obligation. This sense of obligation can also be artificially created by doing something for the other party first and then seeking to cash out, utilizing the principle of reciprocation to your advantage. You could appeal to all sorts of things here—how family always helps family, or that you have done some big favors, so the other party owes you. Take your pick. Ultimately, you are appealing to the idea that the other person is responsible for the consequences that will happen if the victim refuses to go along with things.

Lastly, you can utilize guilt. When the obligation is not met, guilt is felt in response, and people do not enjoy the feelings of guilt. For many, the feeling of guilt can be enough to really motivate them to go along with whatever you are asking for. For example, you could remind your target of how much money you spent on them for some random event, even if the context is skewed in that particular example you are using, attempting to hit all the right buttons to evoke guilt.

Any of these three are likely to be quite effective—you install the strings to these emotions, and pull the strings any time you want or need something, and oftentimes, the individuals follow simply because they have been programmed to do so.

Silent Treatment

This is another simple concept—in the silent treatment, you suddenly stop acknowledging the other person altogether. You do not speak to them, you do not look at them, and you do not acknowledge they exist in any way at all. If they say something, you do not respond. If they walk past you, you pretend they were a stranger.

The purpose behind the silent treatment is to ensure that the other person feels unsettled and displaced—no one wants to be ignored. Ignoring them literally inflicts pain. In entirely ignoring your target, you are activating the same parts of her brain responsible for pain. The act of ignoring someone activates their pain receptors within their brain, regardless of whether the silent treatment is given by an enemy or by a friend.

This means that you are actively negatively reinforcing whatever behaviors that were being exhibited right before the silent treatment began. You are telling the other person, without saying a word, that they are nothing. You ostracize and reject them in that moment, and leave them reeling and in pain, desperate to make it stop. That desperation and pain open them up to you being able to exploit feelings of sadness and anxiety to get the desired results.

Criticism

Manipulators everywhere recognize the power of words. Criticisms, while they can sometimes be useful when they point out active flaws that require work, are also able to inflict pain if they are relentless and never-ending. They indicate displeasure with the current situation or people involved in that situation. Most people do not want to be on the receiving end of displeasure, and when they are faced with it, they do whatever they can to fix the issue as quickly as possible.

This means that if you criticize your partner in some way, such as stating that he or she is not capable of keeping your shared home clean to your standards, the result will be the partner attempting to show you how you are wrong, cleaning up as much as possible in order to prove that the home can be clean and you can stop stressing out so much. Of course, you can then move the goalposts, shifting the standards further and saying how much you hate that he or she does not also cook home-cooked meals regularly for you.

The criticism becomes a powerful motivator—when you use it, the other person feels the need to push past any hang-ups that had caused the criticisms in the first place, and be better for you. Especially when used in conjunction with one or several of the other manipulation tactics that have been discussed, you are likely to see stellar results.

Chapter 8: Dark Persuasion

While covert emotional manipulation is quite dark, utilizing underhanded tactics that get the job done through brute mental force, dark persuasion is much gentler. With dark persuasion, you are not forcing anything—in fact, persuasion encourages the other party to do whatever is necessary and expected through actively wanting to make it happen, not through feeling pressured or obligated to do so. When you engage in dark persuasion, you are utilizing the principles of persuasion in ways that are nowhere near as covert as those in the previous section. This openness has many different uses, however—it means that you are able to gently lead someone else to the decision you wish them to take, and through that gentle lead, you are able to make the other party feel as though they are in control, when in reality, you are behind the scenes after all.

Defining Dark Persuasion

In order to understand dark persuasion, you must first recognize what persuasion on its own is. Persuasion is the act of gently guiding someone to a certain conclusion or belief through several different methods, oftentimes relating to the principles of persuasion, which will be a major talking point of the next chapter. These six principles of persuasion enable you to convince someone to make the decision you want with their own free will. The key here is that they must be the ones to choose without relying on force or manipulation. Persuasion has an air of honesty to it that manipulation does not, and that honesty makes all the difference—when you are able to be honest about what is happening and making the results you are pushing for more compelling, the other person is more likely to do what you want.

Dark persuasion has one further element to it. However—it is dark by nature. In run-of-the-mill persuasion without any darkness, oftentimes, persuasion is done in order to benefit the other person. The entire purpose is to guide or lead the other person to do something that the persuader believes will be beneficial in some way, shape, or form. For example, a persuader may attempt to convince someone trying to buy a convertible when they have four kids, and their last car just recently died into buying a minivan or a three-row SUV that will fit everyone. This is persuasion—the persuader thinks he or she knows better and guides the other person to behave accordingly. This may be done with honest intentions without really paying attention to the bigger picture—the individual may not realize what the processes are, nor the implications of encouraging such behaviors.

In dark persuasion, however, the persuader recognizes exactly what is happening. The dark persuader recognizes how everything is all interconnected. The dark persuader recognizes who the other person is, what the other person needs to remain motivated, how to do so, and recognize exactly how to get the desired result. The dark persuader is not worried about coming across as manipulative or controlling in any way—to him the ends justify the means, something you will hear a lot throughout this book, and he is willing to take any chances necessary to get the desired results, even if that means delving into moral grey areas to do so.

Why People Use Dark Persuasion

Ultimately, people use dark persuasion for much of the same reasons they utilize persuasion or manipulation—there is a result they desire, and they intend to get that result however possible. For the dark persuader, they want to get whatever they are striving for, whether it is getting a relationship with the person they want, or landing the job that pays more money. No matter what the results may be, the dark persuaders are willing to go the extra mile to get it.

Dark persuaders are sometimes influenced or motivated by whatever the proper right behavior is in that particular circumstance. Sometimes, they will feel inclined to persuade someone for the forces of good or in ways that line up with social norms and morals. Other times, however, the uses for dark persuasion are far more selfish and sinister.

However, despite how sinister these motivators may become, they are done in ways that imply that the individual is not interested in getting what they want through brute force. They recognize that people have free will, but they also recognize that the free will that people have is surprisingly fragile and easily swayed—they instead manage to convince people to follow them willingly.

This can be useful in sales, where you cannot completely lie to an individual without risking your job, but you can still stretch the truth somewhat. You are able to twist how you present things, utilizing appeals to emotions and several body languages and communication skills in order to get the desired results. When you come across as more confident and in control, people begin to naturally defer to you, and when you then are able to use an individual's own emotions against them accurately and skillfully, you are bound to persuade the vast majority of those you encounter during your attempts.

Similarly, dark persuasion can also be seen in various forms of media and advertising—anything that appeals to your emotions in an attempt to draw you in so they can then gently lead you toward certain assumptions, conclusions, or results would be a result of dark psychology.

There are nearly infinite examples of ways that dark persuasion could be useful in a wide range of situations with a wide range of people. Because it is no coercive or deceptive, people tend to find it surprisingly effective and often get desired results, especially as they bet better at utilizing the skills encompassed by dark psychology.

Chapter 9: Using Dark Persuasion

With your newfound understanding of dark persuasion and how it differs fundamentally from manipulation, you are able to begin learning methods involved in dark persuasion. However, the most important piece of information you must learn first is the principles of persuasion. These six principles are incredibly valuable—you can use them in nearly every context in order to influence others to be more inclined to agree with whatever you are doing. Have you ever felt a moment where you felt like the situation would be so much more easily managed if you were able to take charge, take control, and ensure that the results you know are necessary are achieved? If you have, the skillset you need is the one within dark persuasion. Now, let us delve into how to utilize dark persuasion to its fullest extent.

Principles of Persuasion

One of the easiest ways to persuade others, whether dark or not, is by utilizing the principles of persuasion. These principles can be used in a myriad of ways, all of which typically culminates in convincing the other person to do whatever it is the persuader is requesting. Those who are particularly successful at utilizing the principles of persuasion are typically quite emotionally intelligent, recognizing the benefits to acting in such a manner, and understanding that being able to sway the behaviors of others is incredibly useful. The six principles of persuasion that can make or break your attempts to persuade and influence others are reciprocity, commitment, and consistency, social proof, likability, authority, and scarcity.

Reciprocity

The first principle of persuasion, reciprocity, plays upon the tendency of people feeling the need to repay favors when they are first given one. When someone does something kind, society dictates that we feel an obligation to repay the other party in some way. It does not necessarily have to be equivalent, but that sense of kindness is necessary. This works for two specific purposes—reciprocity bonds people, exchanging favors back and forth, and also encourages selfless behaviors in the future. In fact, this concept is so incredibly influential, that the best leaders and the most emotionally intelligent naturally appeal to it. Before they ask what someone else can do for them, they first ask what they can do for the other person.

Commitment and consistency

At its root, commitment is any sort of agreement, whether verbal, written, or otherwise given. By giving a commitment, a confirmation of an intention to do something, people are far more likely to be consistent. This is because of their desire to be seen as consistent. Consistency has three important key features—it is valued, it is beneficial to daily life, and it allows for shortcuts through life. With these three keys, it allows for effective decision making and information processing. The principle of commitment and consistency, then, is the concept that when someone gives a commitment, they are far more likely to go through with it. This means that those who have made any sort of commitments are more likely to persuade themselves to go forward with whatever behavior it is they stated that they would do. They self-regulate, ensuring that they are seen as consistent simply because consistency is so important to people.

Social proof

Social proof is essentially peer pressure conceptualized just for persuasion. The idea is that humans are naturally influenced by those around them and that they always want to be accepted by the groups around them, even to the point that they will defer to the actions of the group, no matter how strange they may be. Because people want to be seen as part of the in-crowd, they are willing to do whatever without really wanting to do so simply to be part of the group.

This is the most effective when people are met with a foreign situation in which they are unsure of how to react. If they are out of their element, most people will look around to see what others around them are doing to get an idea of what the proper behaviors in that particular context would be. The decision is therefore influenced based upon what the group around them is doing at that particular moment.

Likability

The next principle persuasion is likability. In simple terms, people are more likely to be persuaded by someone who is perceived as likable. This can be done in several ways—those who are more attractive, for example, are commonly seen as more likable than someone who is less attractive. Similarly, there are three other key components to identifying how likable someone is, or how to become likable to a group quickly and easily. These three steps are:

- **Being relatable:** People naturally like people they can relate to more than those that are difficult to relate to. They are more likely to be persuaded by someone they can relate to than who they cannot.

- **Use of flattery:** People love to feel good, and flattery is one of the easiest ways to do so. People are easily buttered up by those around them if they appeal to flattery. The catch here is that the compliments given must be genuine to avoid coming across as manipulative.

- **Cooperating:** People love those who are working with them. They are far more willing to cooperate if they perceive the other person as attempting to help them. By creating the end result and wording it in a way that the two of you will be cooperating, you are more likely to convince the other person to work with you.

If you can meet these three steps, you are likely to convince those around you to want to cooperate and work toward whatever goals you set out. When you have checked off all three steps, you will be seen as much more convincing than those around you.

Authority

The next principle of persuasion is the appeal to authority. This principle of persuasion states that people are naturally more willing to go with whatever the authority tells them is the best bet. People are willing to concede when they do not know enough to make an informed decision, and in doing so, they defer to whatever they think the authority wants them to do. This means that if you can establish yourself as an authority somehow, whether through utilizing your credentials, displaying any accreditations, or having someone else introduce you with whatever credentials and accolades you have collected over the years, you are far more likely to be successful at persuasion.

Scarcity

The last of the six principles is the principle of scarcity. This is nothing more than supply and demand—if something is readily available and easy to get, people will not see it as valuable. However, as soon as it is restricted in any way, people automatically want it or miss it. Despite the fact that it may have been disliked prior to it becoming scarce, as soon as it was restricted, people saw it as desirable and would feel the need to get it. This means that in order to utilize scarcity, you would need to limit something—you could show how much someone stands to lose by not acting at that moment, or you could threaten to end a relationship, making you yourself a scarce commodity.

Methods of Dark Persuasion

With those principles in mind, there are several different methods that people use to utilize dark psychology. Take a look at some of the most common ones here. Remember, this is not an exhaustive list but encompasses the methods of dark persuasion that you are most likely to encounter during your journey understanding dark psychology.

Leading Questions

Remember, those utilizing persuasion, in general, are ultimately looking for people to reach conclusions on their own. They want to make sure that the people around them that they are persuading feel as though they are acting on their own volition, and utilizing leading questions is no different.

These are questions that typically either imply or contain the answer to the question that is being asked, enabling them to be used as a persuasive technique. For example, imagine that you are selling that car once again. Rather than asking if the person wants to buy the car, you ask a leading question instead, such as, "When would you like to speak to the finance department about this car?" You ask a question that implies that they will be buying the car, and they answer in a way that will tell you everything you need to know to continue with the interaction. If they answer that they are ready then, you know they are dedicated. If they seem wishy-washy about it, they are likely not entirely convinced. Notice the two principles of persuasion that are present here—you can identify commitment and consistency along with an appeal to authority. As the salesperson, you set yourself as an authority figure, and by asking them to name a time that they would like to speak to the finance department, you ask them to make a commitment.

Transference

When utilizing transference, you are using any combination of words, pictures, symbols, or colors in order to create or transfer an emotional reaction to the audience. This can be either positive or negative, creating either positive or negative feelings within the audience and swaying the audience one way or the other. This is most commonly seen in all sorts of advertisements or media, in which the way that the advertisement is designed is meant to sway the consumer into feeling a certain way about the product. This is why commercials are largely so positive or use a certain message that they convey. They want that message to lock into your mind for later use. When you see the item in the store, then, you feel whatever emotions you were feeling during the advertisement.

Obscuring True Intentions

This is sometimes necessary when trying to persuade others. When you obscure your true intentions, you try to emphasize the benefits to those around you while making it a point to sidestep whatever you may stand to gain in the process. Think about it this way—would you really trust a salesperson if they told you, "Hey, yeah, I know you want to buy a house like that, but you know what would be great? If you bought this one over here that is twice the price! Think of all the money it'll get me— I mean, uh, you can enjoy the nice views and the extra space!"

That does not really come across as a good or trustworthy salesperson, although they were honest about what they wanted and what they were getting out of the interaction. When you obscure your true intentions—in this case, making money—you are able to seem more impartial, which can make you seem more like an authority figure.

Moving the Goalpost

One last common dark persuasion technique involves moving the goalpost. This is exactly what it sounds like—you start with one thing that you ask for, and when that is agreed to, you ask for a little bit more. These incremental increases in what you need do not seem that bad when it is only a little bit more work, but by the end, you may find yourself doing significantly more work than you initially would have agreed to.

When utilizing a method like moving the goalpost, you are appealing to the principle of commitment and consistency. You are getting the person to make one small commitment, and then using their desire to be seen as consistent to your advantage as you pile on more and more until you have reached your desired results. By making it incremental, it seems much less daunting to agree to. For example, if you ask your coworker to take care of all your copying and shredding, they are likely to say no. However, if you were to stop your coworker as they walk to the back and ask for them to do one small thing that they agree to and they say yes, if you add another small task to that, they are much more likely to agree than if you would have asked them to do the two things at the same time earlier before the coworker had agreed to anything at all.

Chapter 10: Mind Control

Now, this is where the book gets interesting. When you were a child, did you ever fantasize at being able to literally control the minds of others? Perhaps you thought it would be fun to use others like robots, making them cater to your every whim, or maybe you found it entertaining to think about making someone dance about or do embarrassing things just for fun. The idea of mind control is fascinating to humans, so much so that we make countless movies, books, games, and more about controlling other people. It is a major part of media, even to this day. The concept of taking that control can be exhilarating to some people. While you cannot take complete and utter control of another person's body, you absolutely can take control of their thoughts in a slightly different manner.

What is Mind Control?

If you still have the notion of someone walking around literally controlling someone else with a computer or remote, erase that from your mind before continuing. You cannot do that. However, you can train people to have certain specific reactions and behaviors to certain specific situations. Think of this like teaching your dog how to behave—your dog, if you did a good job, should be well trained enough that you can snap your fingers, say a couple of words, and encourage the dog to do something that you have commanded. You can do something similar to humans, although it is usually much less noticeable than that.

With mind control, you are able to condition another human to have certain emotional reactions to certain stimuli, oftentimes utilizing small movements on your face, hands, or your own emotional state, to get the results that you want. You can essentially tame and train the other person, convincing them to do whatever it is you need them to do without a second thought. You remove their capacity for free will, to an extent, and render them no different than the dog that you can command at a whim.

While this is absolutely possible, it is a longer process. It takes time, and if you try to rush the process, you are likely to end up with a bad result in which the other person either catches onto you and leaves while they still can, or you create poor connections that do not work as effectively as they should be. Think of this like fishing—if you yank back and reel in the fish too quickly, it will get away. If you take too long, you risk the fish eating the bait off of the hook and swimming away before you could catch it. Just like with fishing, you must be able to create a fine line between too much and not enough to get the proper results.

If you do it right, however, you will take control of the other person. You will systematically remove their own thoughts, replacing them with your own that serve you in some way. You remove their free will, establishing all sorts of conditioned responses through all sorts of methods in order to teach them to behave in certain ways. You essentially break everything that made that person a person, and without some serious help, they are not likely to be able to reverse the damages very easily.

Difference Between Mind Control and Brainwashing

Ultimately, when you decide to use mind control, you are committing to the long game. You are essentially assuring that for a while, you will be spending your time subtly training someone else to behave in ways that will work best for you. When you choose to use mind control, you are essentially ensuring that you will gain a position of trust in order to get close enough to be able to install all of those methods you wish to use to create the mind control you desire. This is inherently different from brainwashing in several key ways. Brainwashing and mind control, while they have similar end results, are largely dissimilar in several major ways.

The Intended Target

When you are attempting to control someone using mind control, you are committing yourself to the long process of gaining trust, dismantling the other person's self-esteem and other defense mechanisms, and slowly installing all of the strings that will enable you to get whatever you want from the person. Through these methods, you will find yourself able to do a wide range of things you never thought possible—the person will literally be malleable to you, allowing you to slowly and systematically shift thoughts, shift habits, and shift goals into something that will be beneficial to you in every way, shape, and form.

When you are utilizing brainwashing, however, you are using it against an enemy. Trust does not have to be built or earned as you are not attempting to make the person feel as though you are trustworthy. When you use brainwashing, you do not worry about the other person liking you—you want obedience, and that is it, no matter what the cost. This brings us to the second key element: Awareness.

Awareness of Manipulation

When someone is mind-controlled, they are not aware of what is happening. The entire purpose of using mind control is to manage to make sure it stays covert and undetected. You want to ensure that the other person does not detect what you are doing because you want to be seen as trustworthy to your target.

When someone is being brainwashed, however, they are absolutely aware of what is happening. They know that they are in enemy territory and are aware of the methods that are being used and what the end result will be. This creates a huge key difference between mind control and brainwashing—those who are aware of their brainwashing can oftentimes overcome the brainwashing relatively simply because they understand what was happening as it was happening, and it is easy enough to give up those beliefs. However, those who have been mind-controlled do not realize it is happening during the process. They have a much harder time distinguishing between their own legitimate thoughts and the thoughts manipulated into them.

The Methods Used

The last key difference between the two is the methodology used. When brainwashing is being utilized, the techniques are much more violent and utilizing all sorts of inhumane, dehumanizing methods. Mind control, on the other hand, is far gentler, slowly acclimating the individual to the world of being controlled without ever spooking the other person or causing the person to notice any red flags arising in the process.

Chapter 11: Mind Control Tactics

With a basic understanding of what mind control entails, you are then ready to move on to the tactics involved in mind control. These are particularly dangerous, especially in conjunction with the steps to priming the target for mind control. This is best done when an individual has already had their own sense of self-esteem eroded down enough for them to be relatively malleable. When this is done, they are far more susceptible to the rest of the priming and the techniques that will be used.

Remember, this is absolutely an unethical practice. There is very little way to spin this to be positive in any way. This is always detrimental to the target involved and absolutely can cause irreparable damage if done. Nevertheless, we shall delve into the steps involved in gaining the control of someone else's mind, as well as the methods typically utilized.

Steps to Mind Control

Develop Trust

The first step to set up control over someone else's mind is to develop trust. You cannot mind control someone else without first developing the trust necessary for the rest of the steps to follow without detection. You can do this in several ways; such as utilizing the three keys to likability discussed within the principles of persuasion. You can utilize mirroring and other body languages in conjunction with love bombing or other manipulation tactics to create an artificial relationship. Regardless of how you do it, you must make sure the person you seek to control trusts you.

Destroy the Old Personality

Once you have established the relationship sufficiently, it is time to move on to the next step. Here, you need to essentially destroy the individual's old personality. This is absolutely essential since without this, you cannot create the pseudo-personality that is meant to be loaded up with your own thoughts and beliefs rather than those of the individual you have targeted.

To destroy the old personality, you must convince them that their old personality is flawed in some way. This is why someone with low self-esteem is so much easier to overtake than someone who is confident. When you are able to convince someone that they are inherently broken, flawed, or weak, they are more likely to enter a stage of questioning and doubt in their own identity.

Debilitation

With the individual busy questioning who they are and what they want in life, you are then able to move on to the debilitation stage. While not strictly necessary, especially if the person you are attempting to manipulate was already particularly malleable as an individual, when you debilitate your target, you make them far more susceptible to your own manipulation and thoughts and feelings you wish to install. This can be done through several methods—sleep deprivation, abuse, poor diets, drugs, or even physical or sexual assault. Anything to weaken the person as a whole and enable them to be more easily controlled goes here.

Personality Insertion

Through many of the mind control tactics that will be listed below, you will be able to understand exactly how you can insert the personality of what you want into the other person.

Thought control, such as limiting of choices and repetition and reinforcement could slowly impose your own thoughts and beliefs into the other person, slowly becoming internalized until the other person believes them as well, or thinks he or she believes them.

Testing Your Control

That is, it! With those steps, the other person should be within your control. The particular methodology you will use within each step depends on your particular target. You will need to ensure that the methods you choose to use match up with who you want to control and how you want them to behave. You can now test your control through methods such as testing to see emotional reactions or watching to make sure that you have thoroughly conditioned the person to go through with whatever it is you want.

Methods of Mind Control

Now that you have a general idea of the steps to mind control, you can begin to understand the actual methods used. Take a close look at each of these methods of mind control. Some of these have already come up earlier within the book, and those will be glossed over, discussing only the relevance to mind control in this section.

Repetition and Reinforcement

As briefly discussed earlier, repetition and reinforcement utilize the idea that if you say something to someone enough, they will begin to internalize it. This is what many people use to utilize affirmations, and it absolutely works in the negative as well. Through this method, you can convince other people to behave in ways you never thought possible, simply by inserting your own thoughts into their minds and making them think they were their own. This is perfect for inserting a pseudo-personality to replace the personality of the individual you are controlling.

Limiting Choices Available

Limiting choices available is another way to insert thoughts—you can sway the direction someone is thinking by making them think that they must choose between an artificially created false dichotomy or limited selection. Think of how you can give a child the illusion on a choice through providing them with a few choices that you approve of rather than letting them make the decision themselves, such as asking whether the child wants carrots or broccoli with dinner instead of asking if the child wants veggies for dinner. You can do this with adults as well—by implying that there are only a few choices that are acceptable to you, the other person's thoughts are limited just enough to be acceptable to you, no matter which choice is made.

Sleep Deprivation

When you need to break someone down, sleep deprivation is one of the easiest ways to do so. Through sleep deprivation, with as little as 21 hours being necessary before signs of impairment become apparent, you are able to make someone far more susceptible to manipulation. If you can keep someone awake long enough, you will be able to subsequently control them simply because they are already exhausted and ready to pass out. They are not going to have the mental fortitude to defend themselves.

Emotional Manipulation

Remember the section on covert emotional manipulation? All of that can be utilized when attempting to engage in mind control. Return to that chapter for a refresher if you feel the need to do so.

Isolation

Isolation strips a person of anyone around them that could potentially help them defend themselves from various forms of manipulation and mind control. When someone has a large circle of friends, family, and loved ones who understand them as a person, any subtle changes in personality are far more likely to be noticed early on, calling everything into question. If you can isolate your target, you make it less likely that you will be caught in the process of attempting to manipulate them.

Chapter 12: Mind Games

Some people, no matter the situation they are in, just like to play mind games. It is a way to control another person, essentially turning them into a toy or a plaything that can be used for entertainment and nothing else. When someone is playing mind games with you, you will never be aware of what they are doing unless you recognize the signs. Likewise, if you are interested in playing mind games with others, you need to develop an understanding of the following several techniques.

What are Mind Games?

Mind games are a wide range of actions taken specifically to get certain results from the other person. It is usually meant for the player to have fun gaining control of the other person, seeking to one-up the other person and utilizing all sorts of skills and techniques to develop power.

This can be seen everywhere—in office politics, in relationships, or even with random people out and about. Typically, the person who most intensely moves forward with these games feels an incessant need to justify his or her own power, looking to demean and humiliate others in order to do so simply to get their way. While, especially in workplaces, some healthy competition is important, this typically goes well past that point, seeking instead to dominate others.

In relationships, mind games are utilized as a way to toy with the mind of the other person, essentially in complex forms of gaslighting to make the other person doubt themselves. They are typically quite insidious, and the results are usually the victim becoming incredibly insecure and lacking trust in him or herself.

Why Use Mind Games?

The most compelling reason people utilize mind games is to gain control. In doing so, they are able to do a few different things. They establish themselves as superior, which is major for those who have dark personalities, especially if they fall within the dark triad. By proving themselves superior, they only add an extra layer to their justification that people can be toyed with—if they have proven that they are superior, why can't they toy with the other people?

Beyond that, they are also able to establish themselves as dominant in social interactions. By proving that they are in charge, they are able to assert themselves, taking control of situations, and making sure that ultimately, nothing happens without their say-so, including people being free to think clearly.

These mind games are absolutely detrimental to legitimate relationships, with people within relationships with those who manipulate minds and use mid games oftentimes feeling insecure and unvalued. It destroys the possibility of a legitimate relationship in which the couple can thrive and better each other.

Examples of Mind Games

Ultimately, there are several different types of mind games that people are likely to engage in. These mind games are used for a variety of different reasons, ranging from establishing dominance to simply entertaining the people using them, but what is important is to recognize the ways these games can play out. When you recognize them, you can choose to instead disengage from the situation altogether instead of allowing yourself to continue to be victimized.

Ultimatums

Ultimatums are utilized when someone is demanding a specific result, and if that specific result is not delivered, then there will be intense consequences of some kind. This is often seen in relationships, with one person stating that if some result is not completed, then the relationship is over.

Though some people see this as valid and understandable, assuming people are going to assert their demand for certain treatment without backlash, it is also quite harmful within relationships. While it certainly states a boundary that must not be crossed, and if it is, then the relationship should end, many others use this technique in ways that are meant solely to manipulate the victim, demanding compliance or nothing.

Ultimatums give two choices, do it your way or don't do it at all. It is the epitome of a false dichotomy, with so many more options being available, but those who appeal to it often feel the need to do so to gain control. It forces someone into submission if they value the relationship, and manipulators make sure their victims value them.

In an ultimatum, for example, the manipulator may tell the victim that if they do not learn how to clean the right way and maintain the home properly, then the manipulator will find someone who will. Of course, the manipulator is being unreasonable here—there are several other options here, such as the manipulator helping with the housework or lowering standards, or choosing to hire help elsewhere rather than threatening to end the relationship, but the victim feels pressured—the victim can either call the manipulator's bluff, or try harder in an attempt to do better. Oftentimes, the victims will try to do better, leading to a successful mind game in which the manipulator has asserted dominance and control.

Break Ups

Similar to ultimatums, some manipulators will repeatedly break up with their victims and get back together again, essentially always keeping the victims on edge and worried about the breakup happening again. This keeps the victim insecure within the relationship, and when the victim is insecure, the victim is going to scramble to try to find solid ground. Within the relationship, this means that the victim is going to desperately attempt to gain some sort of stability—the victim will do whatever it takes to make sure the manipulator is happy and willing to say within the relationship, which is ultimately exactly what the manipulator wants. The manipulator *wants* the victim to feel insecure. The manipulator *wants* the victim to feel powerless. And essentially, that is exactly what happens.

The manipulator feels validated then because the manipulator won the game. The victim is left feeling more insecure than ever, which also makes the victim easier to control. To the manipulator, it seems like a positive result all around.

Withholding Attention

Similar to the previously discussed methods of controlling others, manipulators will oftentimes withhold attention from the victim in another twisted mind game. In doing this, the manipulator is able to make it clear that he is displeased with the victim, and the victim is likely to attempt to do anything in his or her power in order to get back in good graces as quickly as possible. In doing this, they retain all of the power—the victim cannot get even basic affection without the manipulator giving it to them willingly, and the manipulator revels in this power as well as the effects of denying it to the victim, watching as the victim desperately attempts to get it.

Silent Treatment

The silent treatment has already been discussed in previous sections, but it is relevant here as well—as a mind game, it is used to establish control over the situation. The punishment will continue exactly as long as the manipulator is willing to make it, and the victim can do nothing to stop it. No matter what the victim does, no amount of begging, pleading, or threatening can do anything to remove power from the manipulator. The manipulator can decide when to speak to the victim, or when not to, and that sort of power play is what the manipulator thrives off of.

Chapter 13: Deception

Have you ever had a sneaking suspicion someone was lying? You may not have understood why you had that belief, but you could not be convinced of the other person's innocence, no matter how much those around you were fooled. Convinced it was just a gut reaction, you probably went on your way without thinking too much about it. However, there is a reason for this—deception can be spotted. You likely recognized some of the most innate signs somewhat unconsciously, allowing your own intuition to cue you in on what has happened. While deception can be effective, it is not always.

This section will define deception as well as provide you with several of the most common deception techniques used in a wide range of situations, from politics to personal. When you know what to look for, paired with your newfound way of reading body language, you are likely to avoid deception from most; only the most skillful will be able to actually deceive you, and even then, you may still be able to recognize the signs after this chapter.

What is Deception?

In as simple terms as possible, deception is lying. It is a technique utilized to mislead others, pushing them away from the truth through a series of different methods ranging from blatant lies to avoid the question altogether. Regardless of the method, deception is largely unethical and something that most people should strive to avoid.

Deception is considered so wrong, so unethical, that it is even possible to sue someone for deception—false advertising. It can be seen as fraud, and even the law recognizes that it can, and should, be punished to protect society. If you are interested in utilizing deception, you should pay attention to the several methods that are commonly utilized, as well as the contexts they are most frequently used within.

How People Deceive

There are several different types of deceptions, and no two are the same. However, all are equally as malicious—they all seek to keep someone from arriving at the truth in some way, shape, or form. That denial of the truth is enough to set off many people, and yet manipulators everywhere still love to lie. They love to utilize it to control others, ranging from gaslighting to other manipulative attempts that require a disconnect from the truth. Take a look at these common forms of deception.

Lying

The most blatant of the way's deception can be utilized, lying involves entirely fabricating a new truth. Rather than just twisting the truth a little bit, the individual is intentionally creating a new answer with the intention of the false information keeping the person that was lied to from discovering the truth. For example, if you are in a situation where you are asked to babysit for your friend, but you really do not want to because you are tired and wanted to spend your evening binge-watching the latest show on your streaming provider while binge drinking cheap wine, you may decide to lie and tell your friend that you are sick. While you absolutely may become sick if you do not mind your wine consumption, you are not sick at that moment—you are quite healthy other than being tired and wanting to relax. You would have been well within your rights to simply tell your friend that you are sorry but you cannot babysit, but instead, you chose to lie about the situation altogether. You created a false truth and fed that to your friend instead of being honest.

Ambiguity

Also known as equivocation, this form of deception involves making answers as indirect, vague, and ambiguous as possible. In doing so, you are able to attempt to veil or hide the truth somehow. This is perhaps most commonly seen in politics, where one person may recognize that their answers would be seen as detrimental to their campaigns to the average person due to how things would be worded. When attempting to hide what their true answer would be, knowing that the media and those who oppose them would twist the answer into something worse, the politician makes the answer vague or ambiguous so it could be understood in several different ways. This means that the politician avoids having to take any real accountability for what is said while also remaining likable to the vast majority of their followers.

For example, a politician may support a new law that will create stringent punishments for texting while driving, but that punishment requires more law enforcement on the road, which consequentially results in an increase in taxes because more law enforcement means more paychecks, which means a need for more money to ensure everyone is paid. When asked if this new law will cause taxes to increase and cost everyone more money, the politician may answer by stating that insurance rates as a whole should drop as the accidents in the area begin to drop as well, and a lot of money will be saved by those who otherwise would have been hit by a distracted driver who was too preoccupied with their phone to watch the road.

Omitting Information

When information is intentionally omitted, some of the truth is left out. While some truth will be told, the deceiver intentionally leaves out anything that they believe may be detrimental to the cause. While some people will attempt to skirt around the answer, others will outright leave information out.

Some people can justify this kind of deception just because they told part of the truth, and they did not lie about anything they said. However, despite being honest, they were still intentionally leaving out important details, and that concealment of important information makes it just as much as deception as lying.

For example, imagine you have just walked into the kitchen and saw your two young children hiding in a corner, with a package of cookies. Both of their faces are covered in chocolate. One child turns around and points at his brother and says that his brother was eating all the cookies, intentionally leaving out the fact that he, too, was also eating cookies as evident by the crumbs all over him. He knows that he ate the cookies, and he never denied it, so in his mind, he has told the truth, even if it was not the whole truth.

Exaggerations

Exaggerations are just that—exaggerating a detail for some reason as if you think it will benefit you in some way to lie about what is happening or what you are doing. You are essentially trying to stretch out the truth to fit whatever narrative you are attempting to sell, such as talking about how bad traffic was because of a massive accident when you were driving to work that day, even if the accident in question was not actually that bad and you were actually late because you were hungover after a long night.

By stretching the truth and exaggerating the effect of the small accident you may have passed, you are deceptive. You are attempting to blame something that was not the cause of your lateness on you being late, even though that is unfair and is avoiding accountability. You may be asking for pity when you are undeserving of it, or you are trying to avoid having to take responsibility. No matter what, exaggerations when meant deceptively are not acceptable.

Downplaying

This is the opposite of exaggerating—when you downplay something, you understate it. You try to play something off as less of a big deal than it actually is. You may have tried to minimize something, so it was easier for the person hearing the truth to accept it, such as claiming that a haircut that was absolutely disastrous was actually not that bad, or saying that someone got a little cut when they needed fifteen stitches to close up the wound.

Despite the fact that people will oftentimes use understatements to be polite, such as to be modest or funny, they are considered largely deceptive, especially when the entire purpose of what was said was to misconstrue what actually happened. If you run into someone else's car and try to tell them that they have no reason to get insurance involved because it is just a tiny scratch when half of their car has a giant scrape across it, you are minimizing deceptively.

Chapter 14: Brainwashing

Brainwashing has already been briefly touched upon during the chapter about mind control, but it is so important and relevant to dark psychology and manipulation, it deserves its own section of the book. When you think of someone who has been brainwashed, oftentimes, the result is someone who is mindlessly obedient, oftentimes out of fear. They may have been kept prisoner for so long that they became obedient just to survive, or maybe they were beaten into submission. No matter what the cause of the obedience, the results of brainwashing are absolutely undeniable—they create someone who is effectively under someone else's control.

Defining Brainwashing

Originally used in the 1950s by Edward Hunter, brainwashing was used to refer to American soldiers that were Chinese war prisoners. Upon release, many different American soldiers declared that they were against Western thoughts and were converting to a communist belief system, which, of course, triggered everyone to fear that the Chinese had actually developed a legitimate form of mind control. In reality, however, those techniques far predated the Chinese and their usage of it in the '50s.

Brainwashing refers to thought reform—it involves several different techniques that, over time, sway a person to change their very thoughts, feelings, behaviors, and core beliefs. They change so much that they have essentially lost their ability to make free choices—they become obedient. The techniques that cause the change can vary greatly, but as a general rule, when brainwashing has occurred, it is typically combined with some sort of danger and threat, with force frequently used.

How Brainwashing Occurs

Brainwashing has several different steps, despite being a somewhat simple concept. In order to brainwash someone, at least in the way that it was done to those soldiers who were studied closely and extensively, there are twelve different steps. Each of these culminates to create a changed person.

- **Assault on the individual's identity:** This challenges the person's identity. People are frequently beaten when answering their questions about their own identities and immediately contradicted afterward. For example, if asked their name, they may answer, get beaten, and then told a new name. They quickly develop doubt about who they are as people.

- **Guilt:** The person being brainwashed is then exposed to massive amounts of guilt, being forced to believe that he or she deserves the treatment being given. It is incredibly important here to make the person feel as if everything is their fault, or if something does not work out just right, then it is on them, and they must feel guilty.

- **Self-betrayal:** This stage involves the brainwashed individual being systematically forced to denounce everything they held dear. Friends, family, religion, culture, and anything else. It essentially culminates in destroying the identity of the person being brainwashed.

- **Breaking the individual:** Eventually, the person being brainwashed recognizes that there is no escape. Without the hope of escape and returning to a previous life, the individual is consumed by fear and the fear of being destroyed, rendering them unable to reason and oftentimes desiring death as quickly as possible.

- **Leniency:** At this stage, when the prisoner or brainwashed individual is certain he or she will break, someone offers a tiny beacon of kindness. The tiniest of leniencies here creates a new hope. This is paired with the manipulator insisting that if the person does as request, then everything can be put behind them, and the prisoner is willing to do so to escape destruction.

- **Compelling to confess:** At this point, the prisoner likely feels a need to confess all sorts of perceived crimes—the point is to cleanse the sense of self in order to allow for progression. The captor, of course, encourages this.

- **Channeling guilt:** The prisoners then begins to feel guilty for his or her very sense of self rather than for the crimes. Everything, involving their beliefs, their family, and their likes becomes a cause for guilt. As they are accepting the viewpoint of their captors, they become guiltier over themselves.

- **Re-education:** At this point, the past identity and everything that went with it is discarded by the prisoners. They are open to reeducation, learning to live with the captor's desires and expectations.

- **Progress:** The more they begin to accept the captors' perspectives and beliefs, the more they are welcomed into society and treated as humans, encouraging them to continue on their path.

- **Final confession:** At this point, prisoners are given one last confession—they are speaking as their new selves that were created by the process and given the chance to clean themselves of their past identity.

- **Rebirth:** Now, the prisoners are recognized as humans once more. They are rewarded for good behavior while punished if they do anything reminiscent of their past lives.

- **Release:** With the process complete, the prisoners are released into the real world, where they are given their rights as humans, but constantly faced with scrutiny for their new identity, or for their old identity, and they are questioned.

Effects of Brainwashing

Ultimately, the effects of brainwashing can be quite dramatic—an entirely new person can be created over a relatively short period of time. This personality is taken as a defense mechanism, happening solely to cling to any form of survival possible to be sure the individual continues to live. By protecting themselves, victims of brainwashing became exactly what those around them desired them to be out of necessity. They knew that the only way out would be through pretending to be someone they were not, even if doing so was denying and rejecting who they were fundamentally as people.

The people are suddenly entirely new entities, much to the shock of those around them, but ultimately, this can be changed. Brainwashing is relatively simple to correct—as soon as people are out of danger, the effects of the brainwashing start to let up, little by little. While of course, there will be plenty of necessary intervention, therapy, and other treatments, the process can be undone.

Chapter 15: NLP

NLP stands for neuro-linguistic processing, which is a combination of several processes of the brain and how they interact together in order to create one cohesive experience. With NLP, you are able to understand the maps that guide the behaviors and thoughts of those around you, and you will be able to tap into those maps in order to manipulate them to something that is more beneficial to everyone involved.

Defining NLP

NLP is one way that people seek to understand the processes of the brain. It allows for people to break down behaviors into smaller, easily understood thoughts, which can then be controlled by the individuals interesting in doing so. Using perceptions of the world around an individual, specific linguistic cues, and behavioral techniques, it is possible to alter the behaviors of the people you interact with.

NLP has a myriad of uses, and is frequently used as a sort of therapy, in which people who would like to change bad habits or create new behavioral patterns are able to tap into their own processing with the help of a practitioner, who can aid in overriding any and all negative behavior and replace it with something more beneficial to the individual hoping to change.

It does this by recognizing the way that how people experience things and think about them can directly impact behaviors. By changing the thoughts, the feelings are changed, and by changing the feelings, the behaviors are changed as well. This sort of domino effect allows for effective use in a wide range of situations.

Using NLP to Persuade and Influence

When attempting to utilize NLP in order to persuade or influence, there are several ways to do so. It is actually built upon persuasion and influence, utilizing the principles of persuasion to influence people to change their behaviors in a wide range of changes. Through utilizing likability, in particular, a practitioner is able to gain access into the mind of a patient and help tweak the behaviors in order to ensure that the individual has more productive behaviors. Here are some of the most common NLP techniques utilized to persuade or influence others.

Mirroring and Developing Rapport

Perhaps the most fundamental skill in NLP is developing a rapport through mirroring in order to ensure that persuasion can occur. While this is a fundamental part of NLP, it is also incredibly crucial in a wide range of other contexts as well—if you learn how to mirror other people, you are able to create a sort of bond between yourself and the other person, which can then be used to influence others.

When attempting to mirror someone to develop rapport, you must follow several steps. The most effective way to do this is through first developing a minor connection—this is done through four steps. First, you front the person, meaning you are facing forward toward them with your entire body oriented toward the other person. Then, you maintain eye contact, but make sure it is a natural amount. Third, you do the triple nod—this encourages the other person to continue speaking while also unconsciously developing a connection simply through agreeing with each other (Remember the principle of likability? You want to like people you can relate to!). Lastly, you tell yourself that you are interested in the other person until you are.

With the connection developed, you can then mimic the pace and volume of the other person, making sure you are matching the other person's vocal cues. If they are loud, you should be loud, and if they are speaking quickly, you should as well.

Third, identify the other person's punctuator—this is something the other person will do for emphasis. Discover whatever that person uses and utilize it in the conversation.

Lastly, test for a connection. If this has been effective, the other person should mimic most innocuous behaviors, such as itching your face or brushing your shoulder. If they do, you have developed a connection or rapport with the other person!

Swish Patterns

A swish pattern is a way that practitioners of NLP tap into the subconscious mind to essentially pivot off of unwanted behaviors in order to completely change the context. Doing so allows for a domino effect that changes the behaviors after changing the lead up to the negative behavior. For example, let's imagine you have a bad habit of biting your nails on a regular basis.

You bite your nails in response to confrontation. When you feel anxious because of a confrontation, you begin to bite your nails—simple, right? When utilizing swish patterns, you will take that anxious feeling, and instead of biting your nails, you will be guided to instead do something constructive, or at the very least, something that is not destructive. For example, maybe you will be suggested to instead run a hand through your hair when you start feeling anxious due to confrontation. While still an outward behavior, it will not harm you in any way.

To do this, the persuader develops the necessary rapport and asks you to imagine the anxiety you feel. You are cued to think about a confrontation with someone, and just as you go to bite your nail, you are subconsciously guided to running a hand through your hair instead through mirroring. The idea is that you can then be guided to completely replace the nervous habit with the less destructive habit over time, creating a much healthier coping mechanism when confronted with confrontation.

Mirroring and Nodding

Once a rapport has been established through mirroring, you can utilize that mirroring behavior in order to subconsciously guide people to say yes to you more often. When you know the other person is mirroring you, you should ask your question that you want the answer yes to and slightly nod your head as you talk. You do not want the nodding to be distracting, but you do want it to be just perceptible enough that the other person begins to mimic it as well. Ask your question while doing this, and then continue the subtle nods while waiting for your response. Oftentimes, the people mirroring you will start to nod their heads in response to you nodding your head simply due to mirroring. However, when they are nodding their heads, they are also more likely to say yes to whatever is being requested just naturally. This is fantastic—you can utilize this in order to persuade people to say yes even if they would normally say no to whatever it is, they want. Try utilizing this in lower-stakes environments to begin practicing and mastering the skills. You would be surprised at just how much you can sway other people through your behaviors and understanding of how their own brains work! In utilizing this, you are likely to get all sorts of yesses—the possibilities are endless. You could do it during a date, when asking permission from a parent, when attempting to get someone else to do something with you, or even on a date or when proposing to a partner! There are plenty of uses for this particular skill, particularly in persuasion and influence.

Chapter 16: Dark Seduction

Have you ever wished you were capable of just looking at someone and drawing their intrigue? Perhaps you have wanted to be able to convince someone else that they want you, perhaps sexually or for an actual meaningful relationship. No matter your motivation, it is a possibility. You can learn the art of seduction, in which people are able to make themselves so alluring, so attractive, that, even if they may not be the most conventionally attractive person at the club or in the room, they can draw all of the people to them seemingly effortlessly.

While this seems too good to be true, surely most of the topics that have thus far been discussed have also seemed too good to be true. Nearly everyone is looking for love and intimacy, and with the skills in this chapter, you will be able to develop both with relative ease.

What is Dark Seduction?

Seduction itself is rooted in the Latin word meaning to lead astray or to corrupt. It is essentially just that—when you seduce someone, you are actively leading them astray, encouraging them just enough to follow you. You are essentially swaying the mind of someone else, encouraging it to want to be with you and persuading the person to be interested in something that would not have otherwise crossed that person's mind. Despite the fact that this has the potential to sound quite inappropriate or dangerous, it is actually important to note the importance of consent involved in seduction.

Seduction is not rape. It is not a way to find victims that you can rape. It is not used as a justification for rape. Seduction absolutely recognizes the free will, and it seeks to make the other person want to freely follow you. You are utilizing your understanding of the human mind and skills you have developed in order to convince the other person that they should want to pursue you.

With that disclosure out of the way, we can now look into defining seduction a little more thoroughly: It is the art of chasing or pursuing someone else until they are pursuing you. You give a little and pull back a little, drawing interest until the other person cannot get enough of you, no matter how hard he or she may try to pull away.

How to Seduce

There are several different methods that you can use to seduce another person. Each of these can be used either together, or separately depending on the results you are looking for. Make sure you spend the time to go over all of the steps within the choosing a target section, as the information there is absolutely crucial to ensure your success in seducing a target regardless of gender.

Choosing a Target

When you are choosing a target, you must be selective. You want to make sure it is actually someone you wish to pursue. Use these three criteria to make sure that you have chosen the perfect target for you.

- **They have attracted you:** Perhaps the most important part to remember is that you must be interested in them. If you are not interested, you are going to lose interest relatively quickly, which defeats the purpose of seduction in the first place. Seduction is essentially the ultimate hunt, allowing someone to enjoy the process of chasing someone down until the other person somehow ends up chasing you instead. In your process of identifying the right target, you must be sure the other person has attracted you.

- **They are receptive to seduction:** Remember, seduction requires the interest of the other party as well. Since the ultimate goal is to get the other person to fall for you, you need to make sure they are receptive to the idea in the first place. This means you must make sure that they seem likely to fall for whatever tactics you attempt to use. If they are not likely to fall for your attempts, they are not going to be very good targets. If they resist too much, forcing it is taking you from a position of seducing the other person to coercing them, which also defeats the purpose of this exercise. Make sure you ride that fine line carefully.

- **They are unhappy with their current situation:** Oftentimes, the easiest targets are those that are currently unhappy. They have a hole in their hearts that can be fulfilled—with you. They are oftentimes miserable with what has happened in their lives so far, isolated and lonely, and seeking more. When you find someone like this, you are then able to snatch them up before they can escape, allowing yourself to have a new pet project. Remember, if the other person is happy with life, they are not likely to fall much for seduction. It is oftentimes the idea of getting something more that draws those who are being seduced in close enough to complete the process.

With your target identified, you are ready to move on to the tactics that are commonly found within seduction. Remember, what comes after choosing the target is largely up to you. You need to make sure you are taking feedback from your target to choose what tactics to use. If your target does not do well with anxiety but thrives on sweet talk and temptation, go for it. There is no one-size-fits-all fix to seduction, and you will have to go through some trial and error to come up with a method that will work for you.

Sending Mixed Signals

When you send mixed signals to someone, they are far more likely to notice you. After all, would you be more interested in another boring person, or someone who seems to be a walking contradiction? At least with the walking contradiction, you are getting something unexpected and new, which can be used to your advantage. You will be exciting and unpredictable, which can draw attention your way, allowing you to scope you're playing field or to target the person you are seeking to seduce, to begin with.

By becoming interesting, you have a far greater chance of success. After all, people are more interested in things that are interesting by virtue of it being interesting, to begin with. Try to mix things up—you may seem really interested in sports and being seen as a general muscle head, but you could also really enjoy romance movies, even if that is a lie. It is okay to embellish the truth sometimes when relying on seduction—it enables you to draw in the people you are attempting to attract, which is ultimately exactly what you are seeking to do in the first place. Be hard and cold, but sensitive at heart, or perhaps you are snappy, but also sweet when you want to be. No matter what the combination, you will find something that works for you.

Cause Anxiety

If people who are content in life become uninterested in the act of being seduced because they are already feeling fulfilled, you can shake things up by inducing anxiety in your target somehow. While it is easier to just choose a target that is already naturally anxious and missing something in life, sometimes, you discover a target that you simply must have, no matter how much you may realize that it will be a challenge. In those cases, you are likely to want to induce anxiety somehow.

Make sure this is done covertly. The best ways to do this will involve the chapters on covert emotional manipulation and mind control—there are several suggestions within that chapter that will aid you in triggering anxiety in someone else.

Make Yourself Look Desirable

When you are trying to make yourself look more desirable, you want to do two things—first, you want to appeal to the principle of scarcity. If everyone seems interested in you, there will clearly not be enough of you to go around, so to speak, and the target you are pursuing is likely to see you as far more interesting. If you have that many people chasing after you, after all, you must be interesting or worthwhile.

Beyond that, you can make yourself look more desirable by making sure you are projecting exactly what you think the other person would like to see and hear. If you know the target is interested in music, take on the other person's interests as well.

Sweet Talking

Remember love bombing? Bring it back here. Offer plenty of sweet talk to keep the other person attracted to you and interested in continuing with the relationship. People love positive feedback, and this is one way to draw the target back in, especially following a low period.

Temptation

People are suckers for temptation—if you can show someone what they could have, making sure it is something you know they would actually like to have, you are likely to see positive results. By giving your target just a glimpse or just a taste of what you have to offer, you are likely to win more interest.

Insinuations

By developing the ability to insinuate comments without actually saying what you mean out loud, you are able to develop further control over your target. You are able to create uncertainty, which breeds anxiety, which leads to a more readily seduced target for you after the fact. Keep this in mind for effective seduction.

Suspense

You want your target to always be unsure of what is coming next. You want them to be so incredibly captivated by you and how spontaneous and surprising you may seem at any given moment that you are always on his or her mind. By maintaining that sort of interest, you will start to see a turnaround in which the target starts showing more of an active interest in you instead.

Make It a Rollercoaster

Your attempts at seduction should not be a smooth ride by any means—you need plenty of highs and lows that will enable you to keep control over the other person. This is done through making sure that you have fun at times, making the relationship seem happy and fulfilling, only to suddenly plummet into a low completely unexpectedly. When you do this, you shake things up—you also make the high points in your relationship seem so much better when they are compared to the lows. Essentially, you are artificially creating a lower threshold, which makes your attempts at actually trying, seem that much more fascinating.

Stay Persistent, but Not Too Persistent

Perhaps the most important reminder for you is to know when to quit. You need to recognize that sometimes, what you are doing is a lost cause and is not worth the added effort. While several people will be open to seduction, not everyone is, and when you encounter someone that you think will be receptive, but after several attempts, clearly is not, it is time to cut your losses and move on to someone else. Do not bother with wasting your time—you will regret doing so.

Why Seduction is Dangerous

While seduction is a fun game for some, anything that is inherently sexual has dangers, ranging from health issues to unintended pregnancies that tie you to someone who was meant to be a fling over a weekend for life.

Beyond the obvious, however, seduction can be dangerous. You are not likely to discover a long-term partner through such manipulative means, and many people would consider this immoral. Ultimately, however, the morality of your sex life lies with you, and you alone.

Seduction is often used by men alone, and is even more common with those possessing the dark triad personality types. It is a viable, albeit not a very effective reproductive strategy. While before, it would have been quite viable, today, it will lead to someone slapped with several cases of child support.

Chapter 17: Avoiding Dark Psychology Manipulation Tactics

While you have now been armed with several different manipulation and coercion strategies, it is time to move to the last portion of this book—defending yourself from the tactics dictated within this book. You may recognize that several of the techniques taught all hinged upon remaining undetected as they were utilized. Simply understanding the techniques now allows you to recognize when they are being used. Your own knowledge on the matter is your first line of defense against such manipulative acts. As you do move on, however, keep in mind these several tips to keep yourself from being vulnerable to manipulation in the future.

Recognizing the Signs

As already briefly mentioned, recognizing the signs of being manipulated is always a fantastic way to defend yourself from further victimization. If you recognizes shifts in personality, for example, or that relationships are weakening, you may be in a relationship with a manipulator. Likewise, if you see those symptoms, or a lack of control, is a friend of yours, it may be worth having a conversation to make sure everything is okay within their life.

Always Defend Your Boundaries

Your first line of defense against any and all manipulation attempts will be your own personal boundaries. These are basically invisible lines in the sand that you draw between yourself and everyone else, depicting several behaviors that you absolutely will not tolerate being violated by anyone and everyone. These boundaries are absolutely reasonable to enforce, despite what anyone else may be willing to tell you. If you have someone else telling you that your boundaries are unreasonable or too strict, it may be a manipulator attempting to convince you to drop your guard to take a chance at manipulating you further.

When you have boundaries, they are designed to ensure that no one is stepping on your emotional toes. They protect you from things you are not interested in confronting or putting up with. For example, some healthy boundaries include not wanting to be cheated on, not wanting to be physically or emotionally hurt intentionally, expecting honesty, or deciding that yelling has no place in the relationship. All of those are rational, reasonable boundaries, though many other manipulators would attempt to convince you otherwise.

When you have set your boundaries, you should make sure that you do not back down upon them. They should be inflexible—if the manipulator attempts to cross one, create a consequence, whether it is walking away to protect yourself or otherwise disengaging from the situation altogether. You are well within your rights to protect your boundaries from the attempted manipulation of other people—they are there to protect you, and you should protect them just as fiercely to ensure they can do their job properly.

Identifying Motives

When you are trying to identify whether you are being manipulated or someone is simply misguided in their attempts to help you somehow, you should always stop and reevaluate their motives. Are they legitimately trying to help you somehow? Do they think they know best, even if it seems like their attempts are poorly guided? Are they being entirely honest with you? Does whatever they are attempting to convince you to do benefit you in any way?

The biggest difference between legitimate, innocent persuasion and manipulation is the intention behind it. When attempting to identify which of the two it is in order to understand how to proceed from that point on, ask yourself three simple questions.

What is the intention of the other person? Is it innocent and legitimately meant in good faith, or is it meant to get something that the other person wants?

Is the other person being truthful with you in that particular moment?

How is this going to benefit you? How is it going to benefit the other person?

While it is entirely possible for persuasion to benefit both people involved in the action, it should absolutely be focused on the person being persuaded, benefitting them more. Of course, the persuader is going to attempt to convince you that it is in your best interest no matter what—if they are being truthful, they legitimately are acting in your best interest. However, the manipulator wants you to believe that you are actually benefitting, even if the manipulator is benefitting far more.

Remaining Assertive

You must always remember to remain assertive with those that attempt to steamroll over you. You should always be the best advocate for yourself that you can be—after all, no one will be able to do the job as well as you can. If you are able to remain assertive, even in the face of someone attempting to manipulate you, you are going to be okay.

Remember, the manipulator wants an easy target. If you are resisting and being assertive, you will quickly get scratched off of his shortlist of potential targets and go off to bother someone else. Your assertion of what you want and need will become too great of a deterrent for you be an effective, easy target.

While remaining assertive, remember what you are entitled to—basic human decency—and never settle for anything less. You deserve to be happy. You deserve to be healthy. You deserve to be unharmed. You deserve to be able to trust yourself. You deserve to be respected and allowed to speak your mind.

Developing a Strong Self-Esteem

When you develop a strong self-esteem, you create one that is far less likely to be eroded away by the manipulator's various methods to degrade you down to nothing. The manipulator wants your self-esteem weak, as that self-esteem is your armor—it ensures that you will be protected when push comes to shove. Those with higher self-esteem tend to trust themselves more, and in trusting their instincts, they are more likely to remain unscathed when a manipulator comes to town, seeking out new victims.

You can do this step several different ways, but one of the most crucial is remembering to recognize your basic human rights, as well as reminding yourself that you are enough just the way you are and that you deserve to find someone that will recognize that you are enough without changing yourself. If you can do that, you will be prepared to tackle the manipulator head-on, avoiding falling for his spells.

Maintaining Close Relationships with Others

Remember, manipulators want you alone. They want to isolate you to remove any safety nets you may have built up over the years. If they had it their way, you would be entirely alone with no contact to the outside world aside from the manipulator. Luckily, life is not often like that, and you are free to contact who you wish. Make sure that you maintain close relationships with those in your life that you value, as they act as a secondary defense against manipulation.

If you notice that your relationships seem to be struggling, or that people in your life seem to be becoming less inclined to speak to you left and right, it is a sign that you should probably take a step back yourself and reevaluate your relationships. It is possible that you have a manipulator in your life attempting to isolate you somehow. If you are able to identify that someone is doing this, you can better protect yourself, actively engaging with people that have started to pull away to reach out for help if you need it, or to reach out to rekindle the relationship that is starting to fade away. You can also ask if there is something wrong and see if they have any answers that could help protect you in the future.

Minimize Contact with Suspected Manipulators

When you suspect someone is a manipulator, the best thing you can do is minimize all contact with that person. Understand that manipulators manipulate, just as rattlesnakes bite and bear attack those who come too close to their cubs. It is simply a fact of life—those with a propensity to manipulate are likely to continue to do so, no matter what. The best thing you can do is entirely disengage yourself completely from the situation, defending yourself and making sure that you are not close enough to be hurt by the manipulator's tactics and attempts to control you.

Remain Firm in Your Convictions

Never give up your convictions or core beliefs for anyone, including manipulators. Regardless of how good they are at trying to convince you to do so, no one who truly loves or cares about you will intentionally try to get you to give up on those most personal thoughts that make you who you are. They would recognize that you have a right to any thoughts and feelings you want to have and that you are more than welcome to create the narrative you want in your own life.

If you notice that someone has been incessantly trying to chip away at one particular part of your life, you may want to stop and analyze the situation, double-checking that it is not a manipulator attempting to get you to do something in particular and instead is someone who is well-intentioned. Even if it is someone well-intentioned, no one should ever be attempting to force you to change what you believe in any situation or circumstances.

Recognize Your Worth

Recognizing what you are worth to yourself and your loved ones is absolutely crucial in protecting yourself from a manipulator. Those who seek to manipulate you want you to internalize that there is something inherently wrong with you. They will intentionally seek to install a sense of shame or that you are not quite right in order to control you later. If you believe that you are faulty in some way, you are more likely to be constantly attempting to fix that flaw that you perceive instead of recognizing that you, like most people, are simply imperfectly perfect the way you are. It is normal and human to have flaws—understanding what they are is absolutely a strength, but only if you can accept those flaws without the incessant need to fix it whenever you pay attention to it.

Remember, your friends and family absolutely love you the way you are, flaws and all. If someone else does not, they are not right for you.

Take Advantage of Time

When someone is actively attempting to manipulate you, repeatedly attempting to get you to give in, the best thing you can do is take advantage of time. Reclaiming time frames puts the power back in your hands—after all, the manipulator cannot do anything without you giving him or her permission.

For example, if the manipulator has been incessantly trying to get you to sign over a car to him because you got a new one and do not need the old one anymore, you can stop the entire situation by telling him that you need some time to think about it. This works with salespeople too, allowing you to take the break you need to disengage from the manipulation and regain control of the situation.

Taking time also allows you to take the time to ensure that any emotions that may have been clouding your perception of what was going on have had a chance to clear. You will be able to consider the perspective through a clear mind without your emotions attempting to sway you to behave impulsively and emotionally.

Saying No

The number one skill that will protect you from the manipulator is being able to say no consistently and firmly. When you are able to tell the manipulator no in no uncertain terms, making it painfully clear where you stand on the matter, the manipulator will have no choice but to accept your answer or risk looking incredibly petty and pushy to those around you. Of course, some manipulators will not care and will incessantly continue to ask you anyway simply because they can. They think they can wear you down over time, especially if they have won out through sheer persistence before, either with you or with someone else. That persistence can be enough sometimes to get them what they want, and they will not hesitate to put it to work if they think they may stand a chance in doing so.

Conclusion

Congratulations! You have made it to the end of *Dark Psychology Manipulation!* Hopefully, as you read this book, you found plenty of information that would serve you well in the real world. While the information provided within this book is solely for informational purposes and you will require real-world practice in order to develop the skills necessary to be successful at reading and manipulating others, as well as making sure that you protect yourself, there should have been something for everyone within this book. Remember, this book does not condone unethical or abusive material, and it was not the intention of this book to be used in unethical or abusive fashions.

Within this book, you were provided with several different topics. You learned all about dark psychology, starting with defining the art of dark psychology, as well as learning what those who use dark psychology tend to look like and how dark psychology is frequently used in everyday life. You were given information about the insidious dark triad personality type, learning essential information about Machiavellianism, narcissism, and psychopathy, all of which play essential parts in manipulating other people. You learned how to read people with several different expressions, movements, and positions provided for you in easily understood language. You were taught about covert emotional manipulation and the tactics used within it. You learned about Dark persuasion and the tactics used within it. You learned how to control minds, brainwash, play mind games, and more. You learned about deception, NLP, and dark seduction. Lastly, you were given information to arm yourself against other manipulators out there in the world. Ultimately, you are bound to run into others who understand this information, regardless of whether their knowledge is innately born or learned over time, and being able to protect yourself is crucial.

From here, you have several options. You can continue your journey learning about dark psychology, in which perhaps you would find an interest in looking into dark subliminal psychology or books that dedicate more time to teaching particular skills that you are interested in mastering. You could alternatively move on to begin practicing the skills within this book on those around you. However, if you choose to practice these skills, do not forget about ethical treatment and that you need to treat those around you with the same basic human decency that you would like to be treated with yourself. You could also give up on your study of dark psychology if you have decided that this is not for you—that's okay! It is not for everyone. Not everyone can stare into the lion's den and remain confident they can stay there unscathed. Regardless of the choice you make, however, thank you for taking the time to read this far. Hopefully, you finished up this book with some sort of useful information that will serve you well. And as this book comes to a close, remember, the ends do not justify the means, and when you begin to treat the human beings around you as nothing more than a means to an end you desire, you are setting yourself up for a lonely life without meaningful relationships. Respect others and use the skills in this book responsibly.

www.ingramcontent.com/pod-product-compliance
Lightning Source LLC
Chambersburg PA
CBHW070133260726
48658CB00001B/398